Ms Muffintop's

Fantasy Sweetheart Collection Vol. 1

Adult Coloring Book

Dear Customer,

Thank you!!! For purchasing my book! This is my very first coloring book! Thank you for joining me on my journey of life and being an artist. The best is yet to come.

Love XOXO Ms. Muffintop

* Upon enterning my lovely world...

*This book is made for coloring

*The pages can take heavy coloring, BUT put a safety sheet behind the page you are coloring . Just in case!!!

*2 copies of each coloring page!

*Single use pages!

*Color test pages!

Ms. Muffintop's

Color Test Page!!!

Test your colors here!

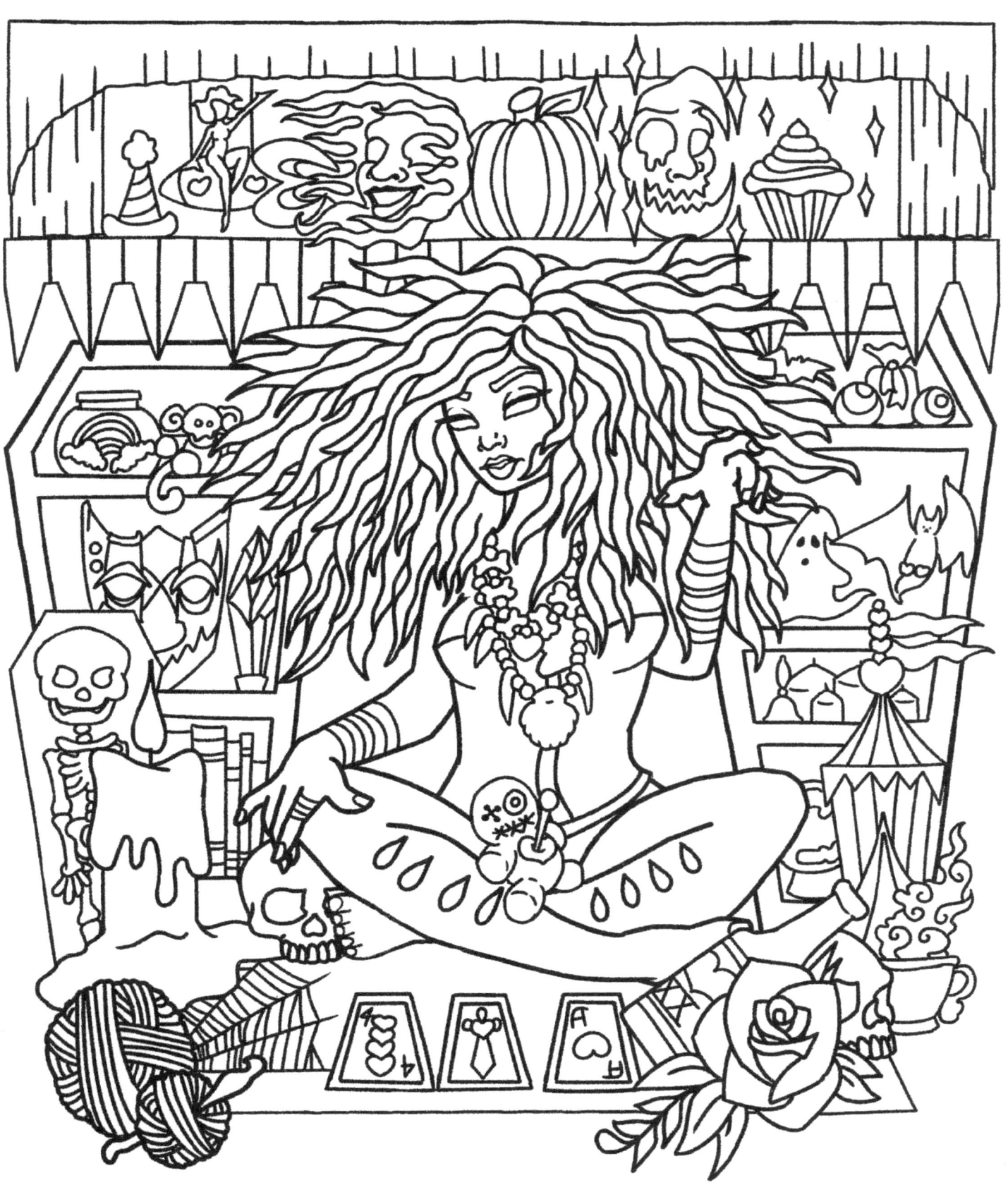

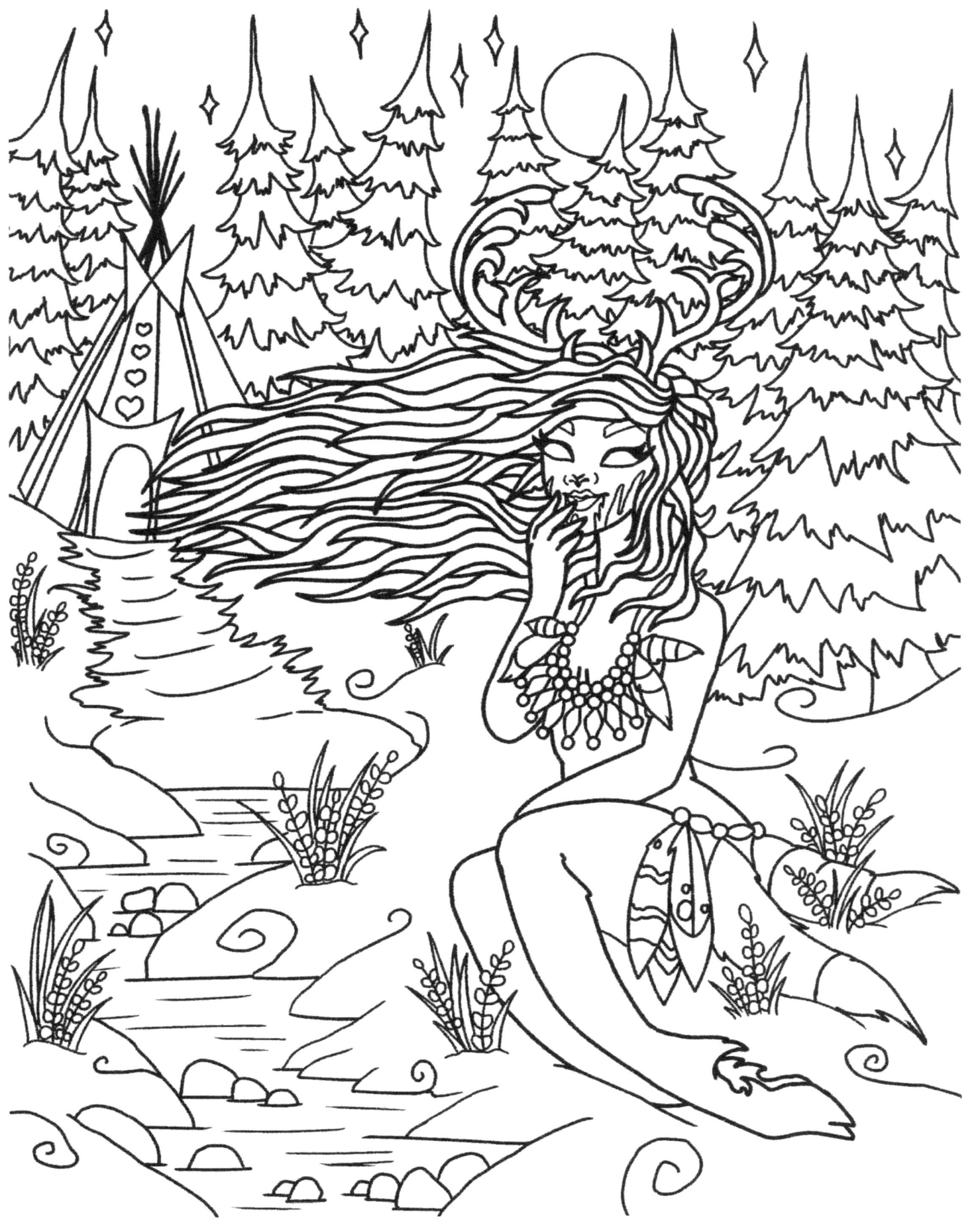

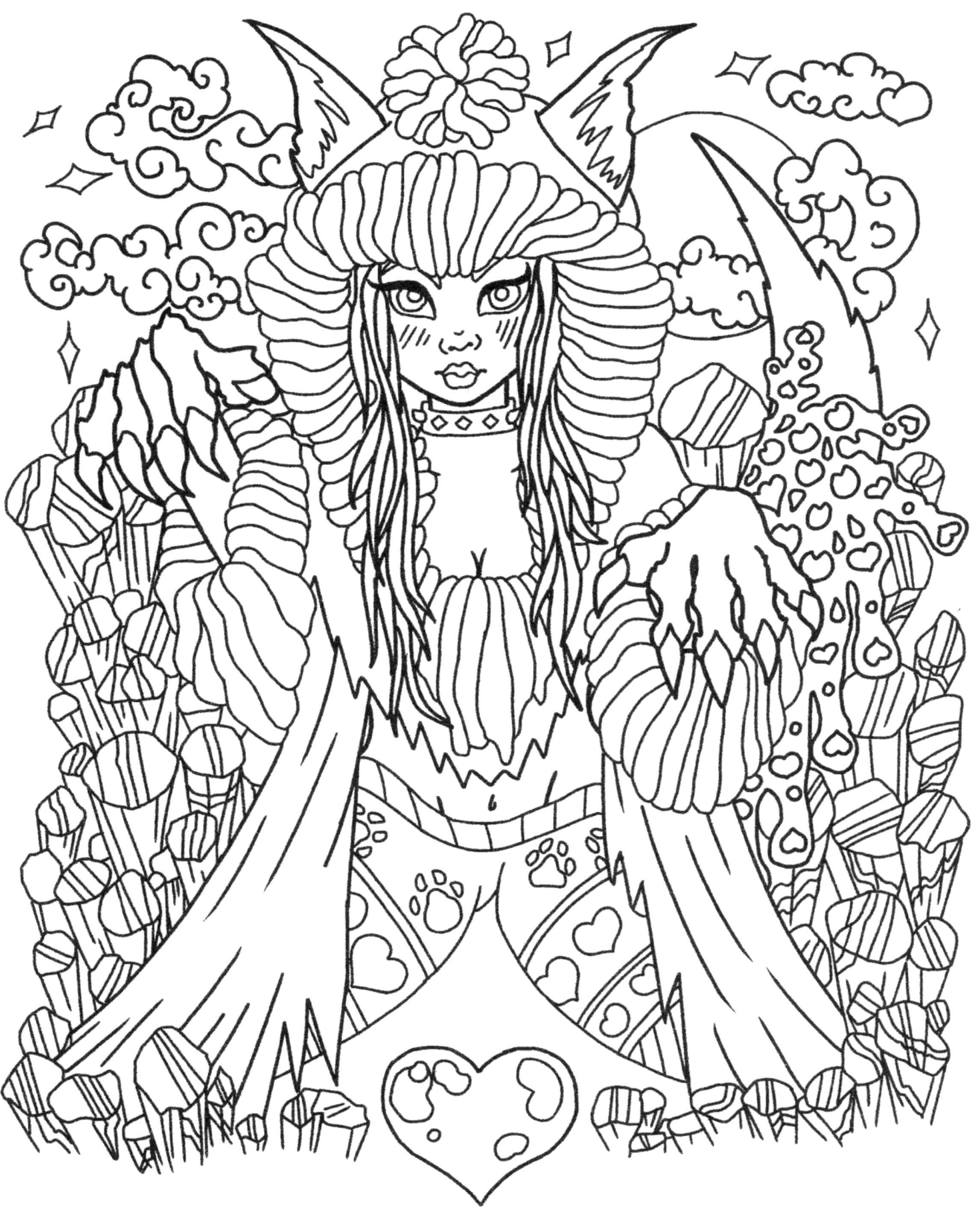

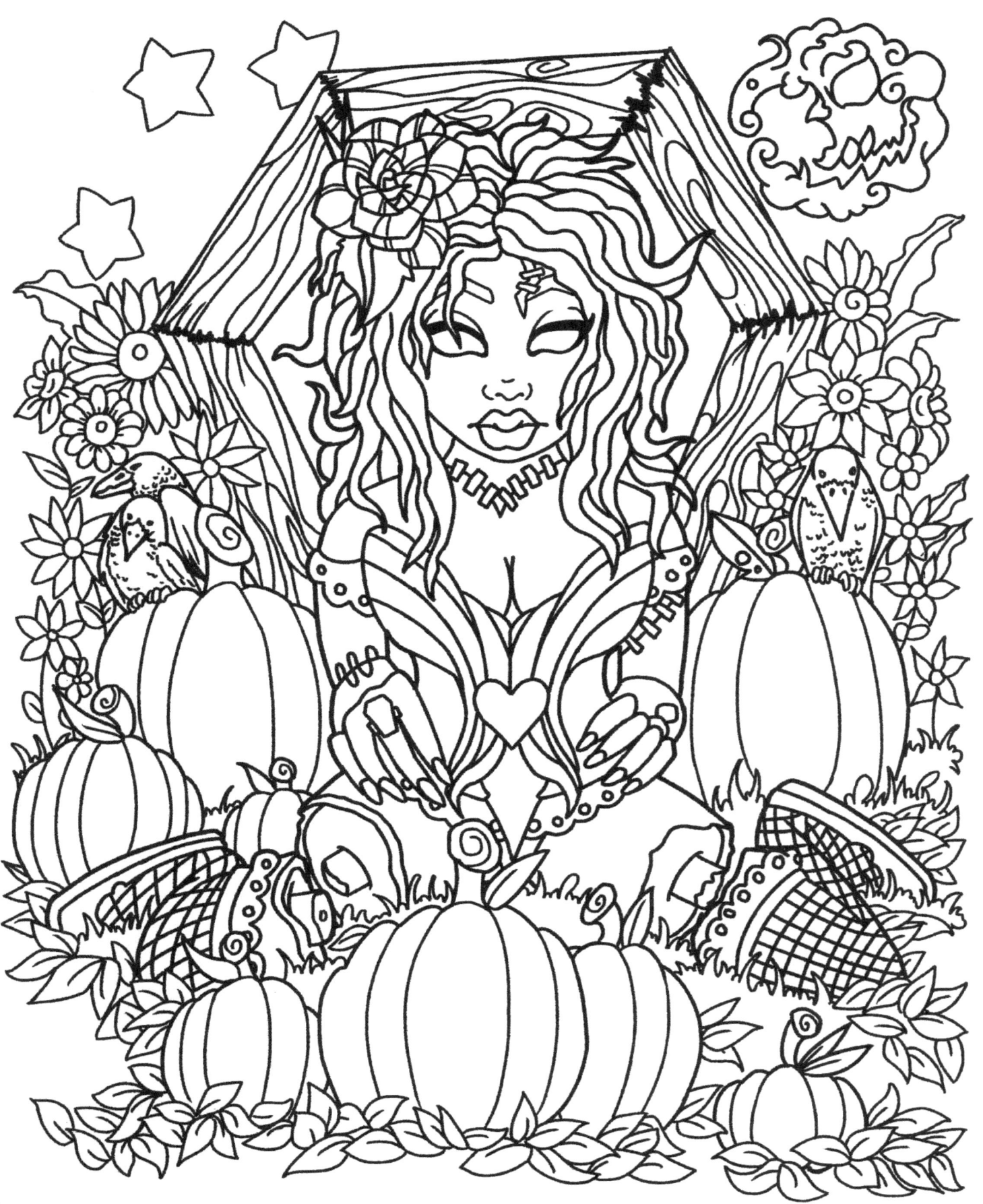

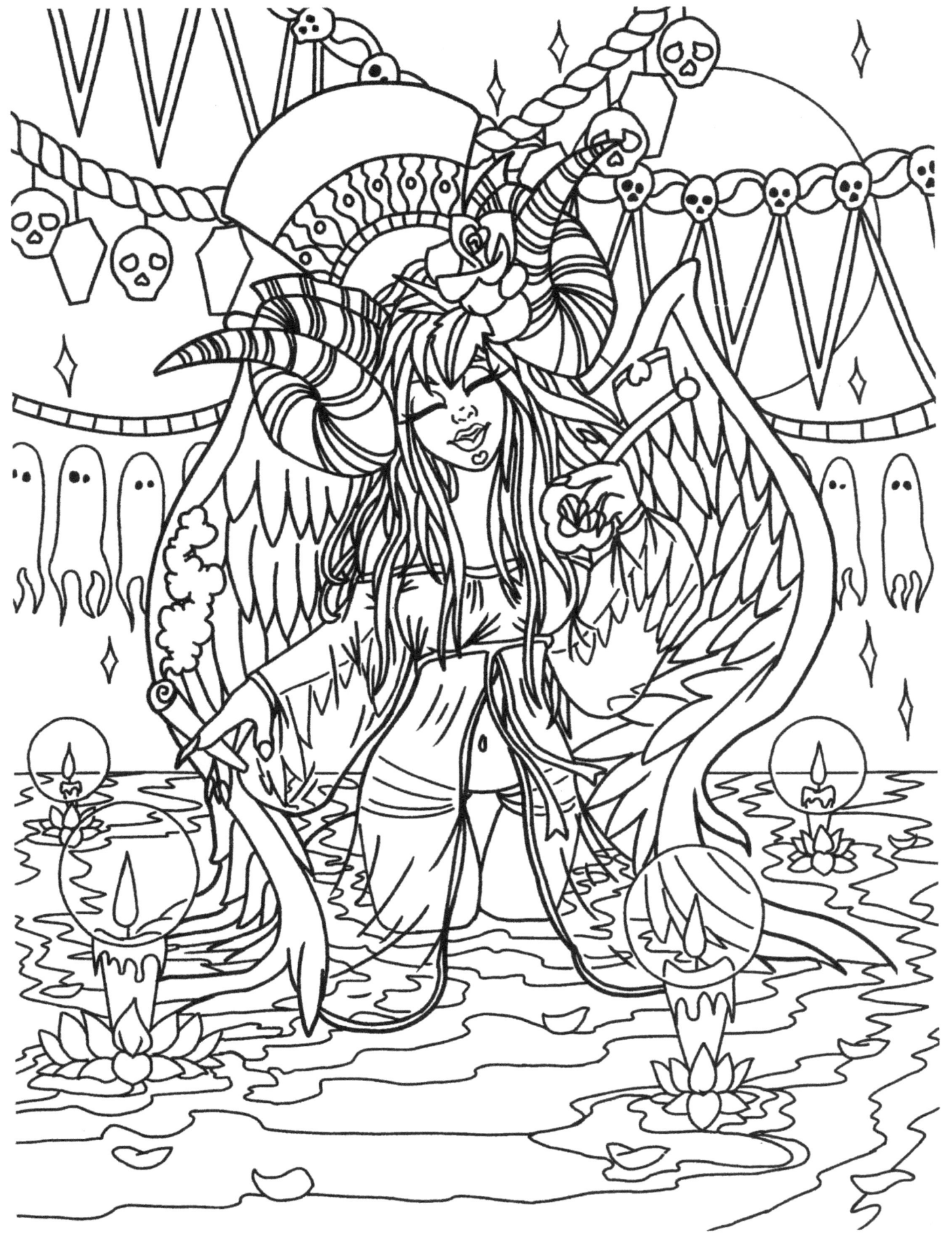

Ms. Muffintop's

Color Test Page!!!

Test your colors here!

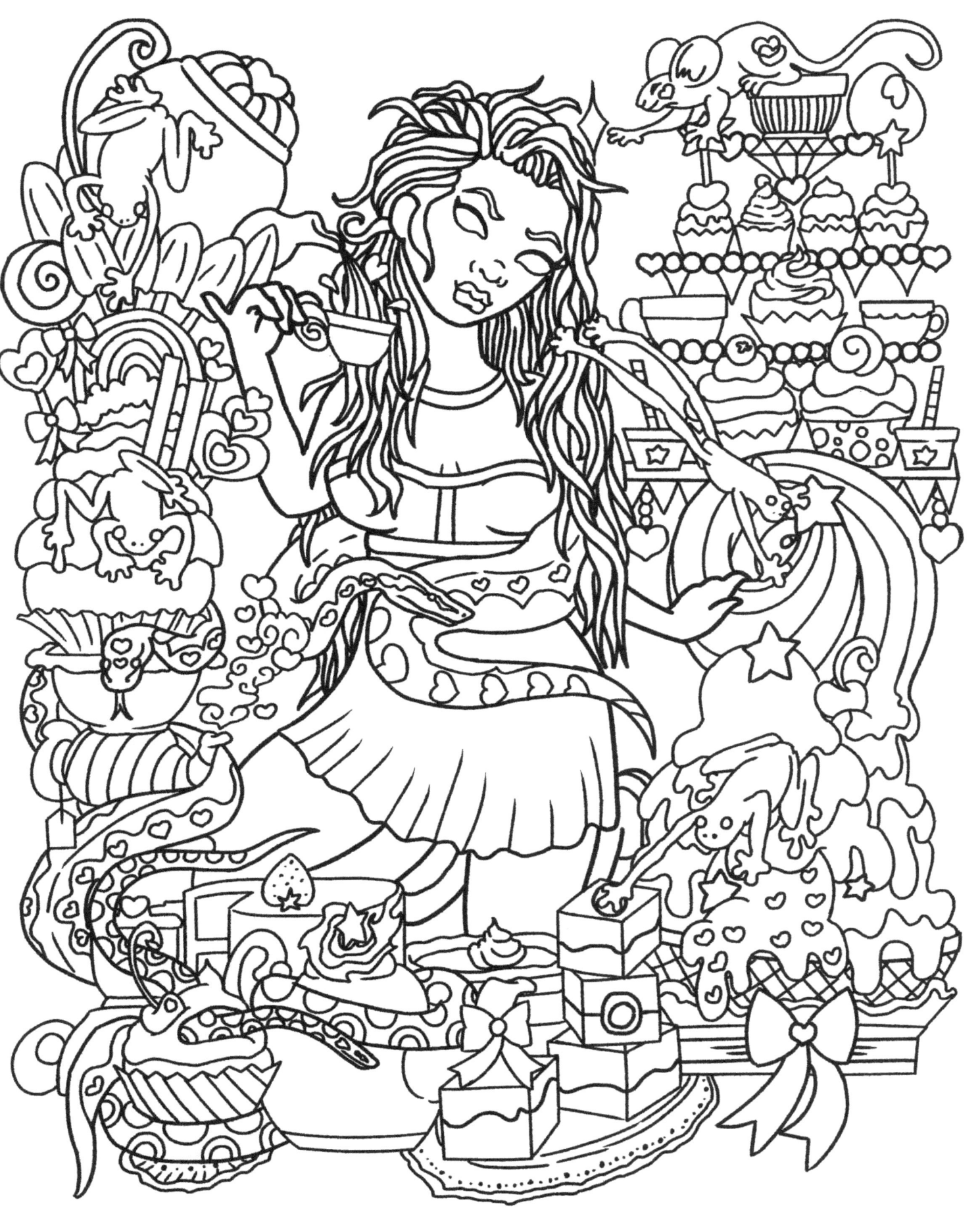

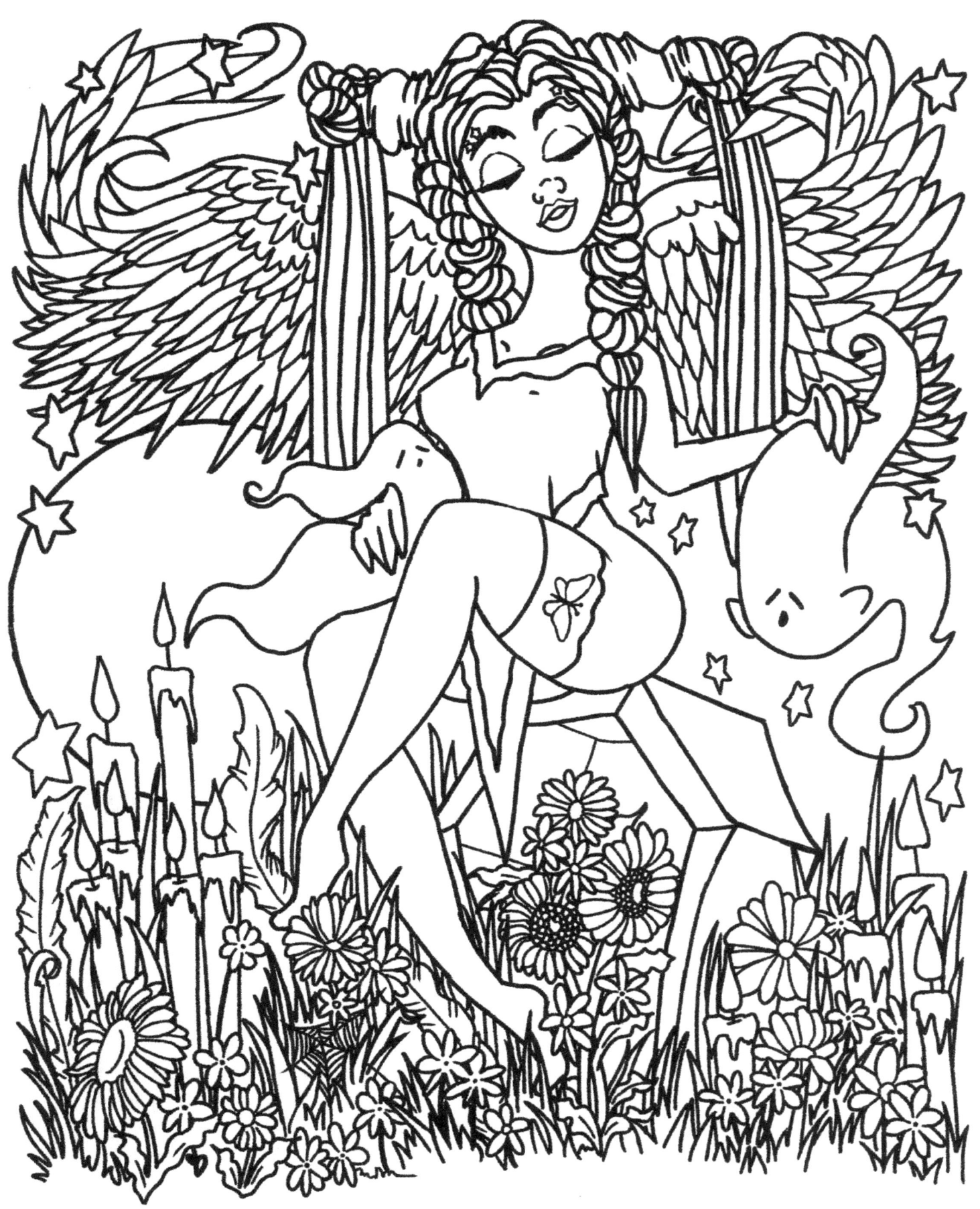

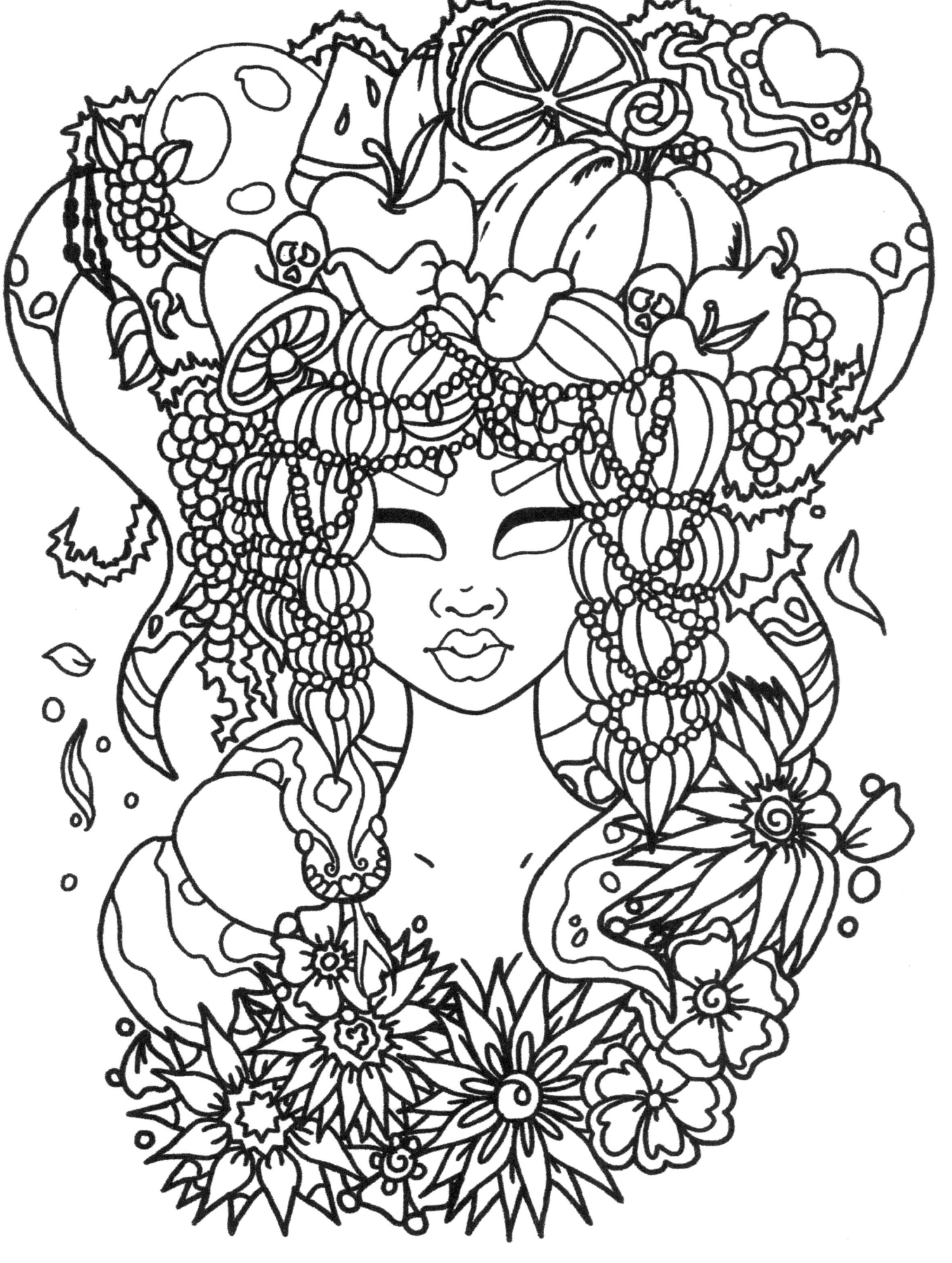

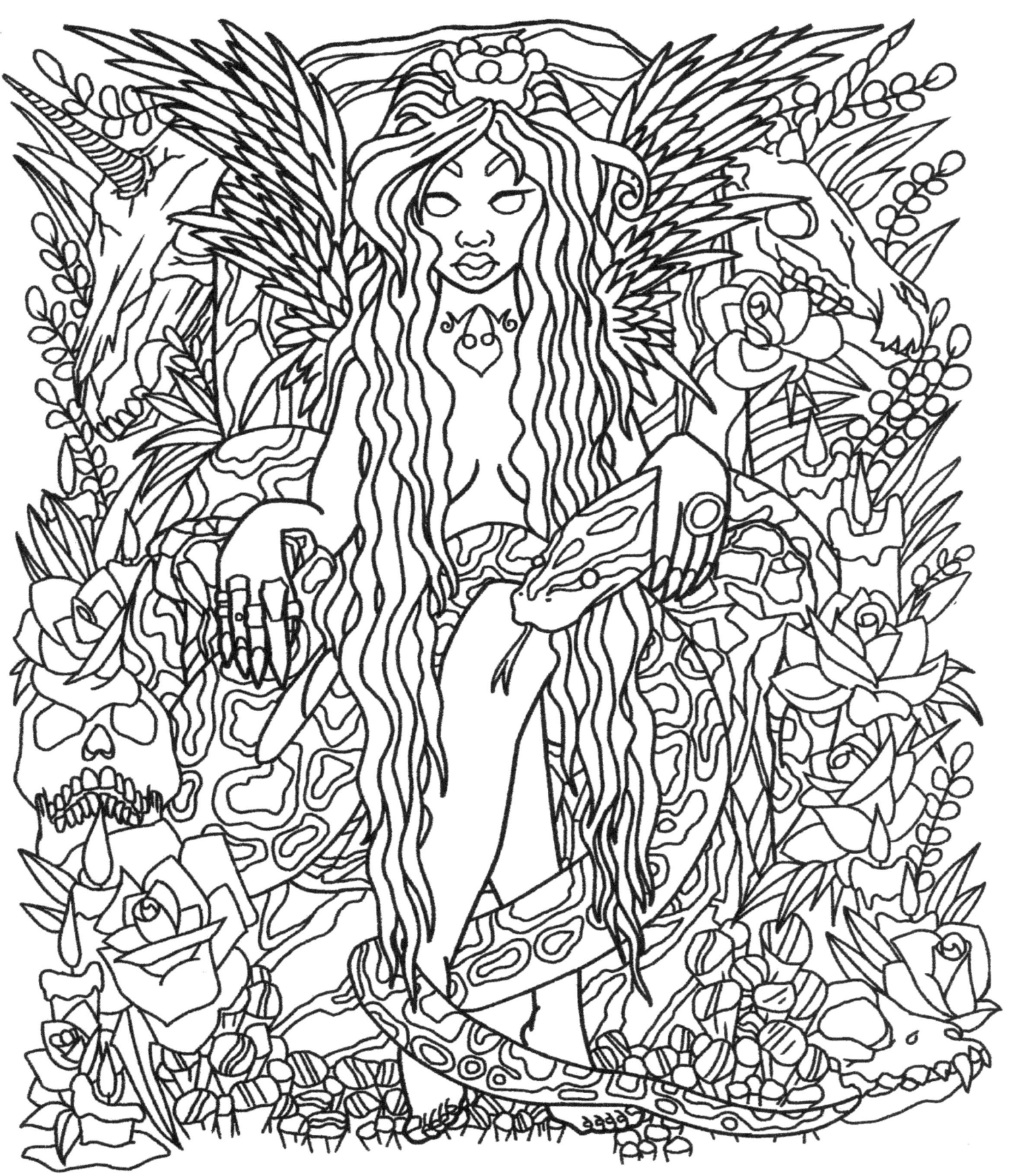

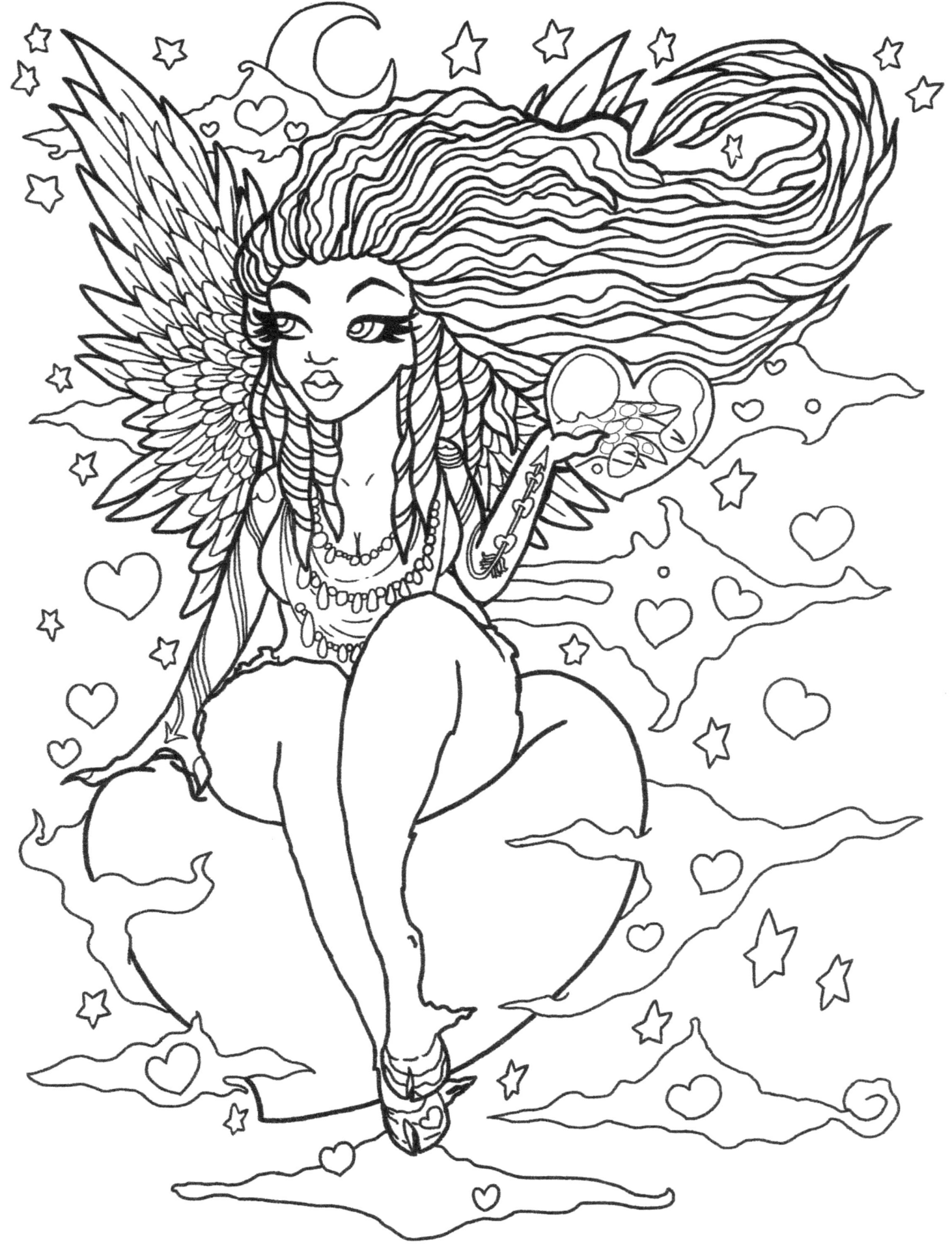

Ms. Muffintop's

Color Test Page!!!

Test your colors here!

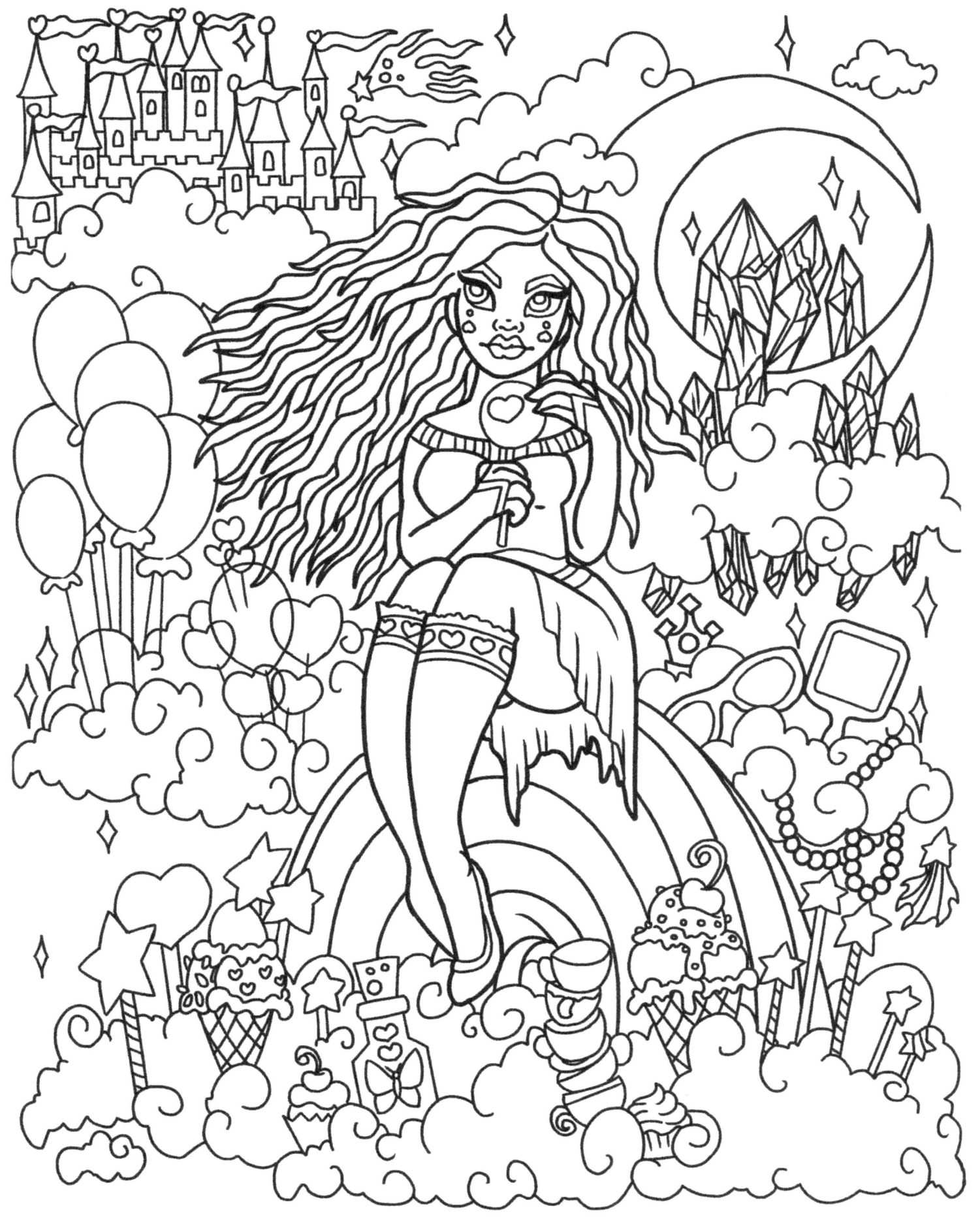

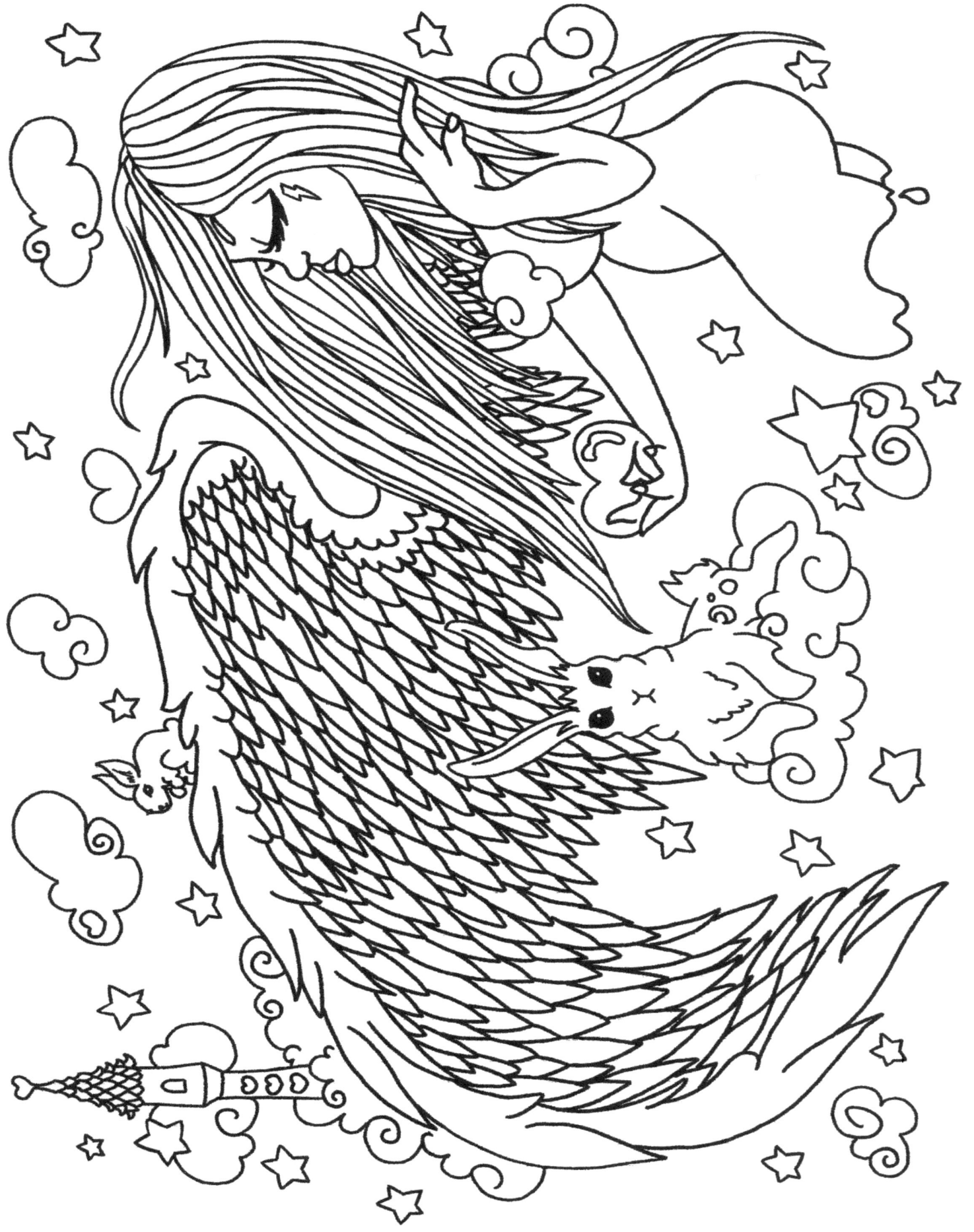

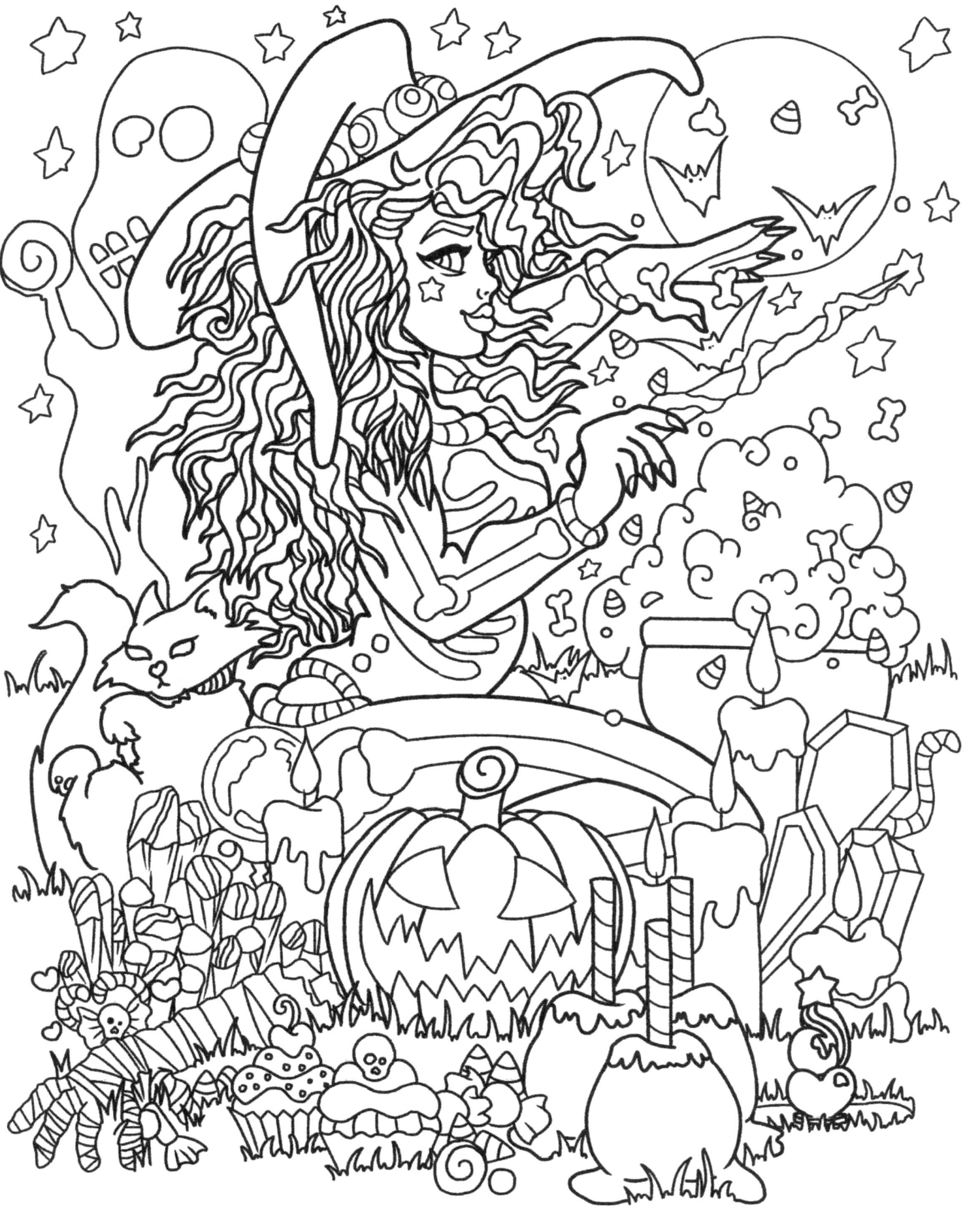

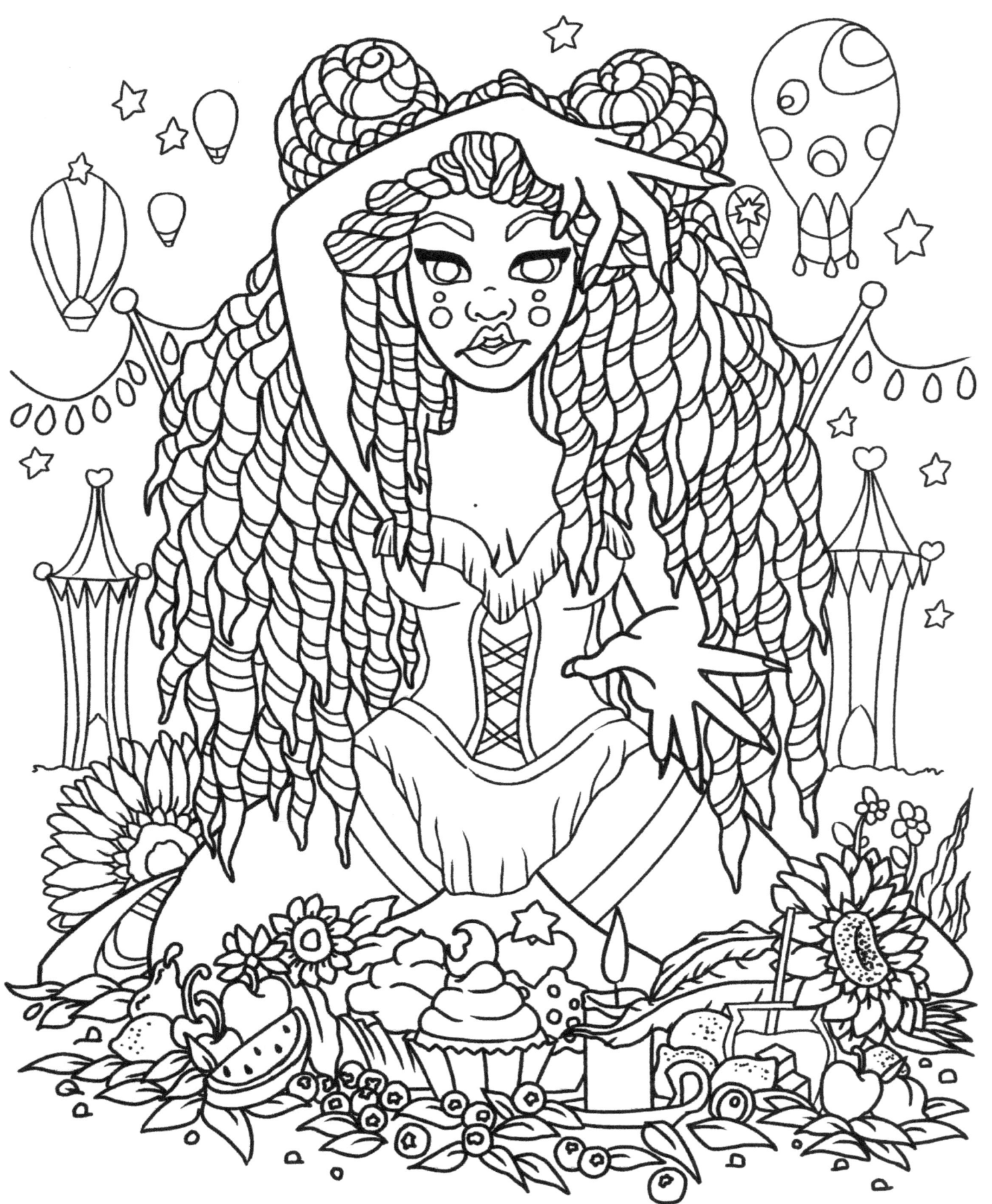

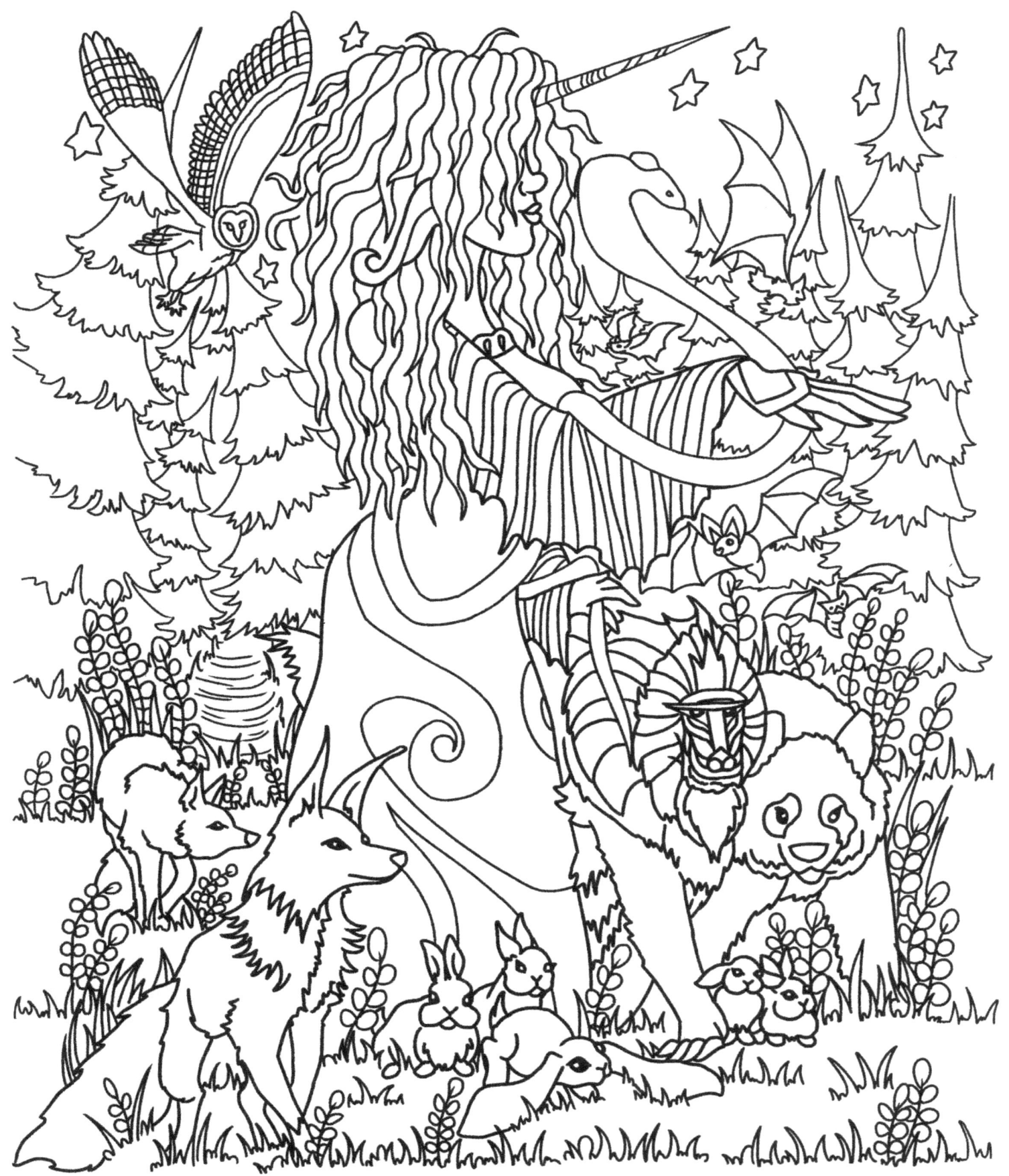

Ms. Muffintop's

Color Test Page!!!

Test your colors here!

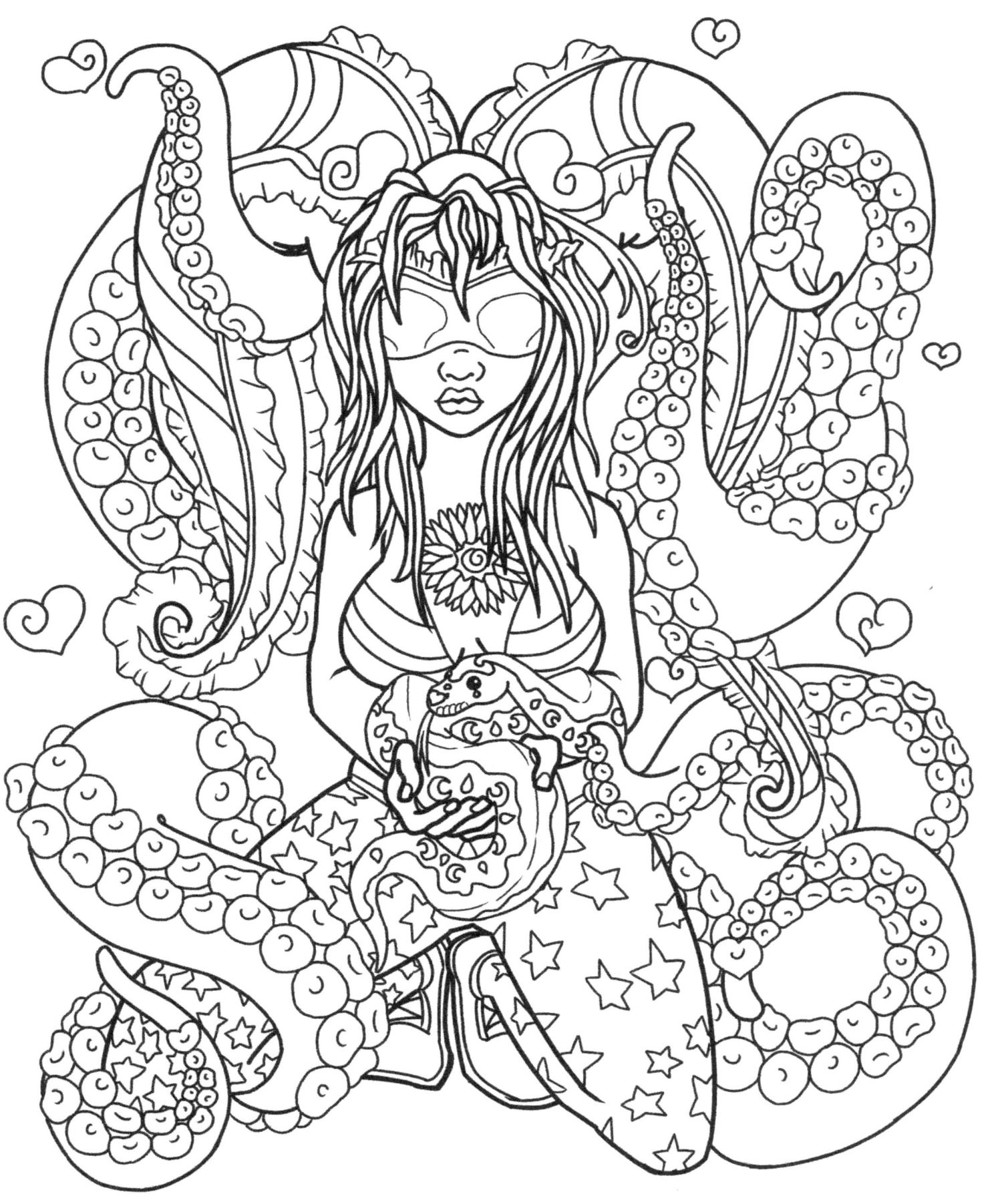

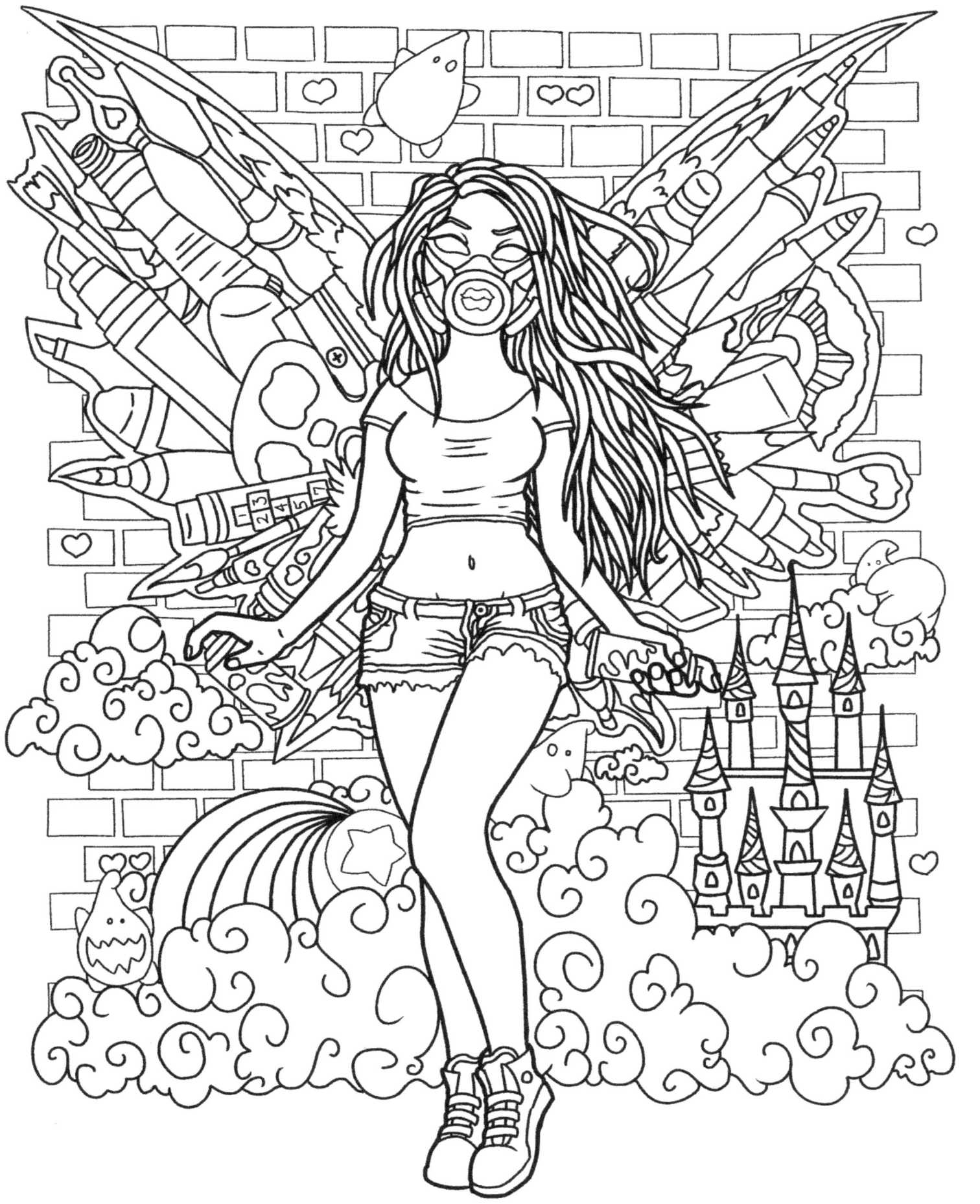

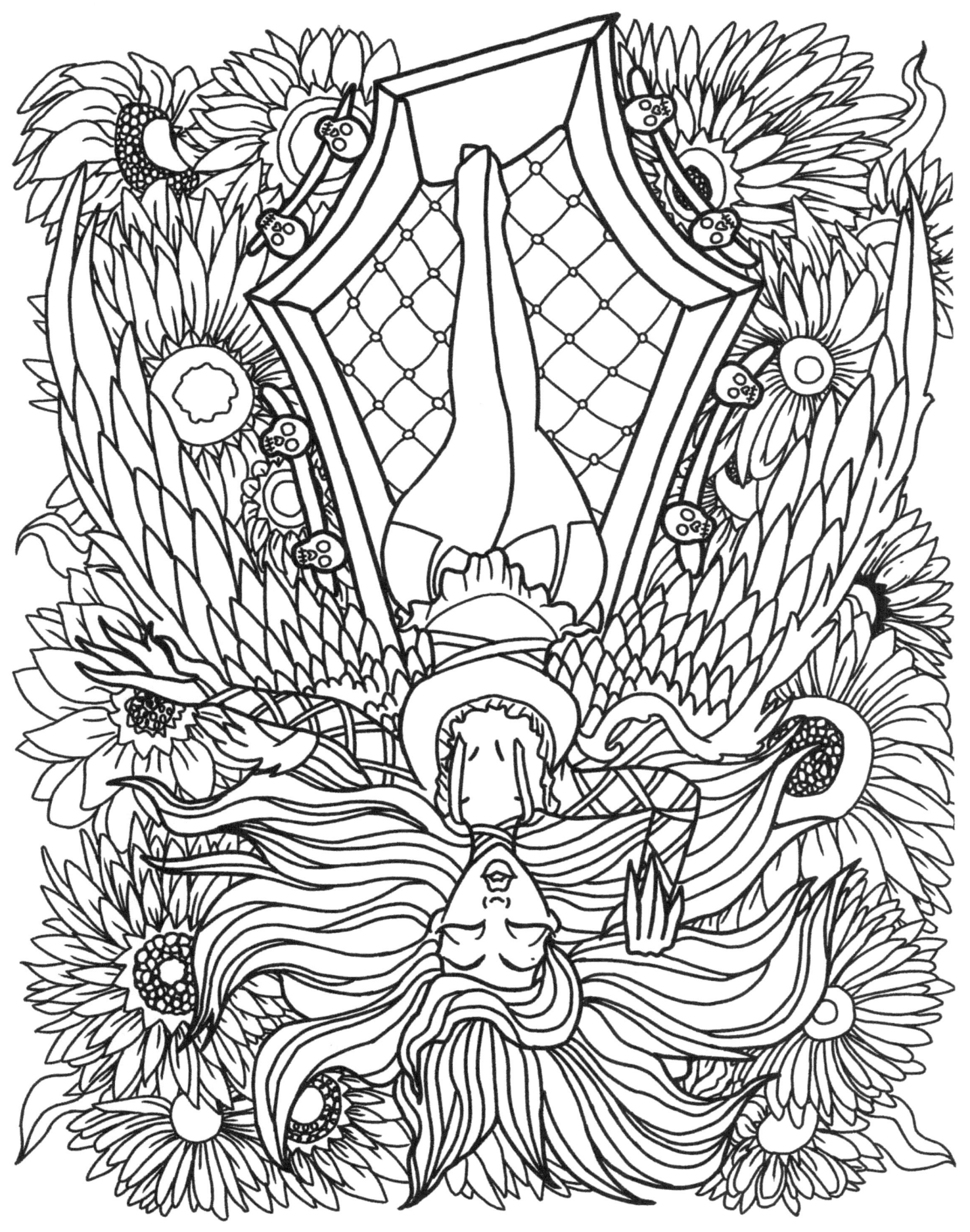

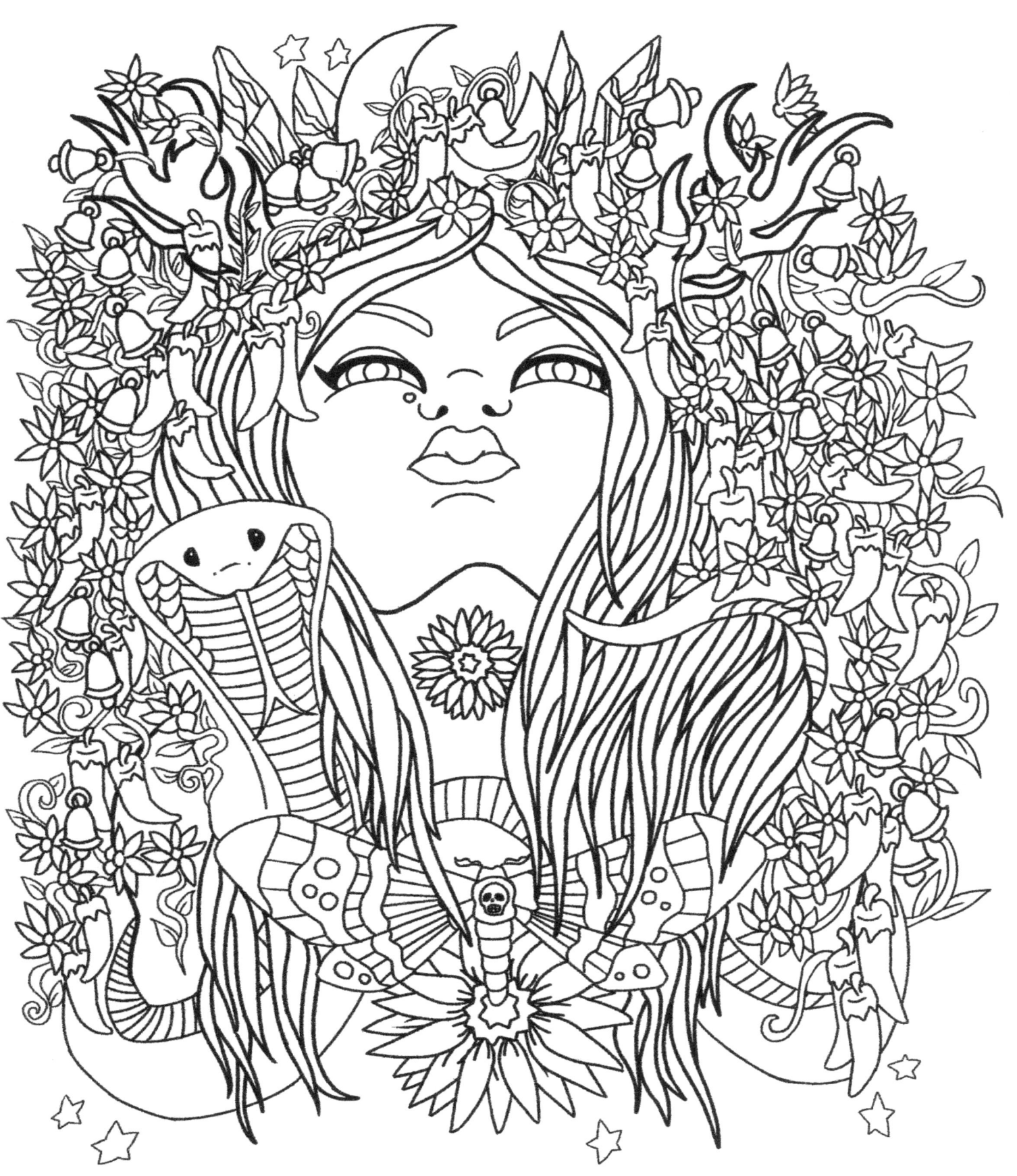

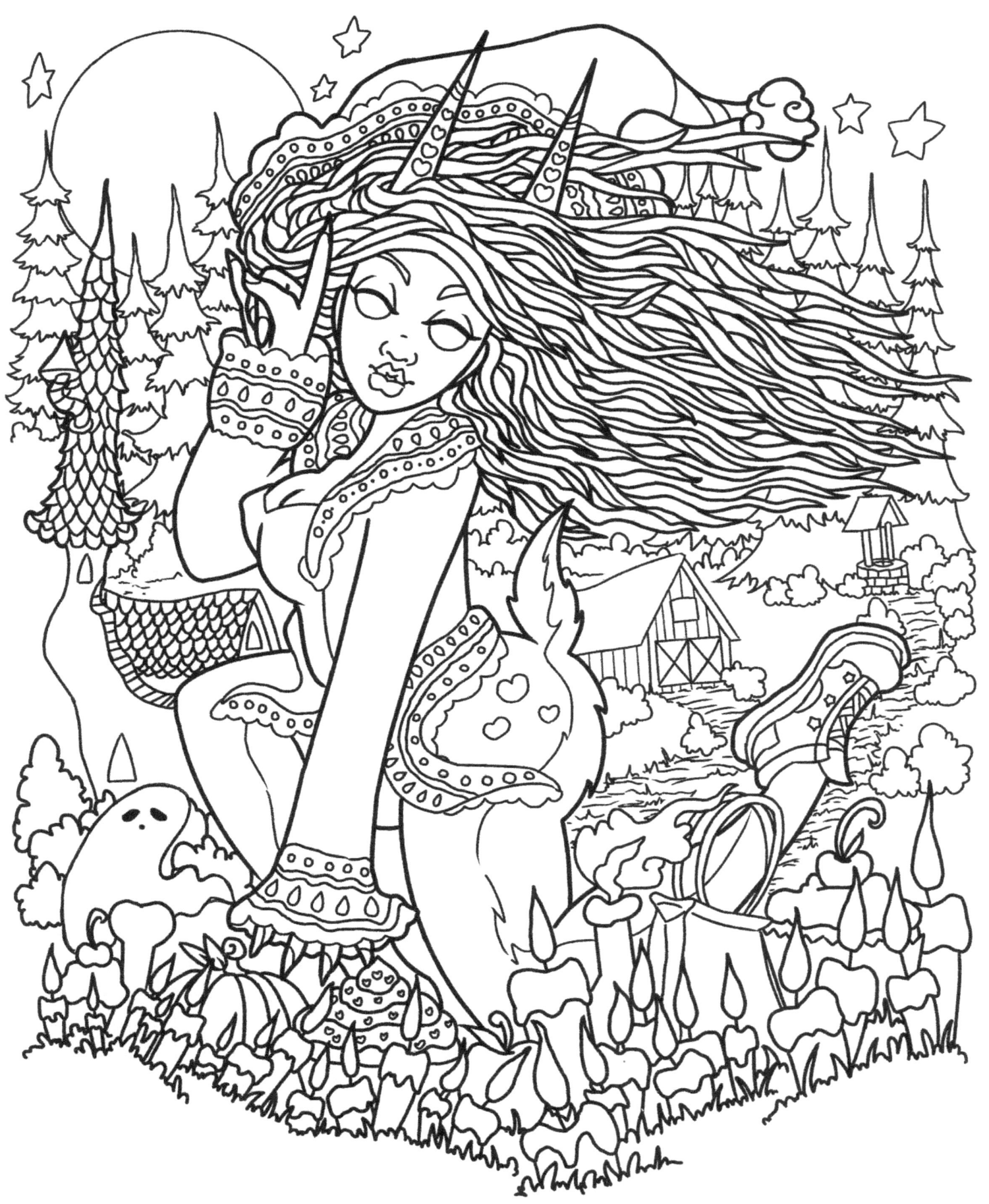

Ms. Muffintop's

Color Test Page!!!

Test your colors here!

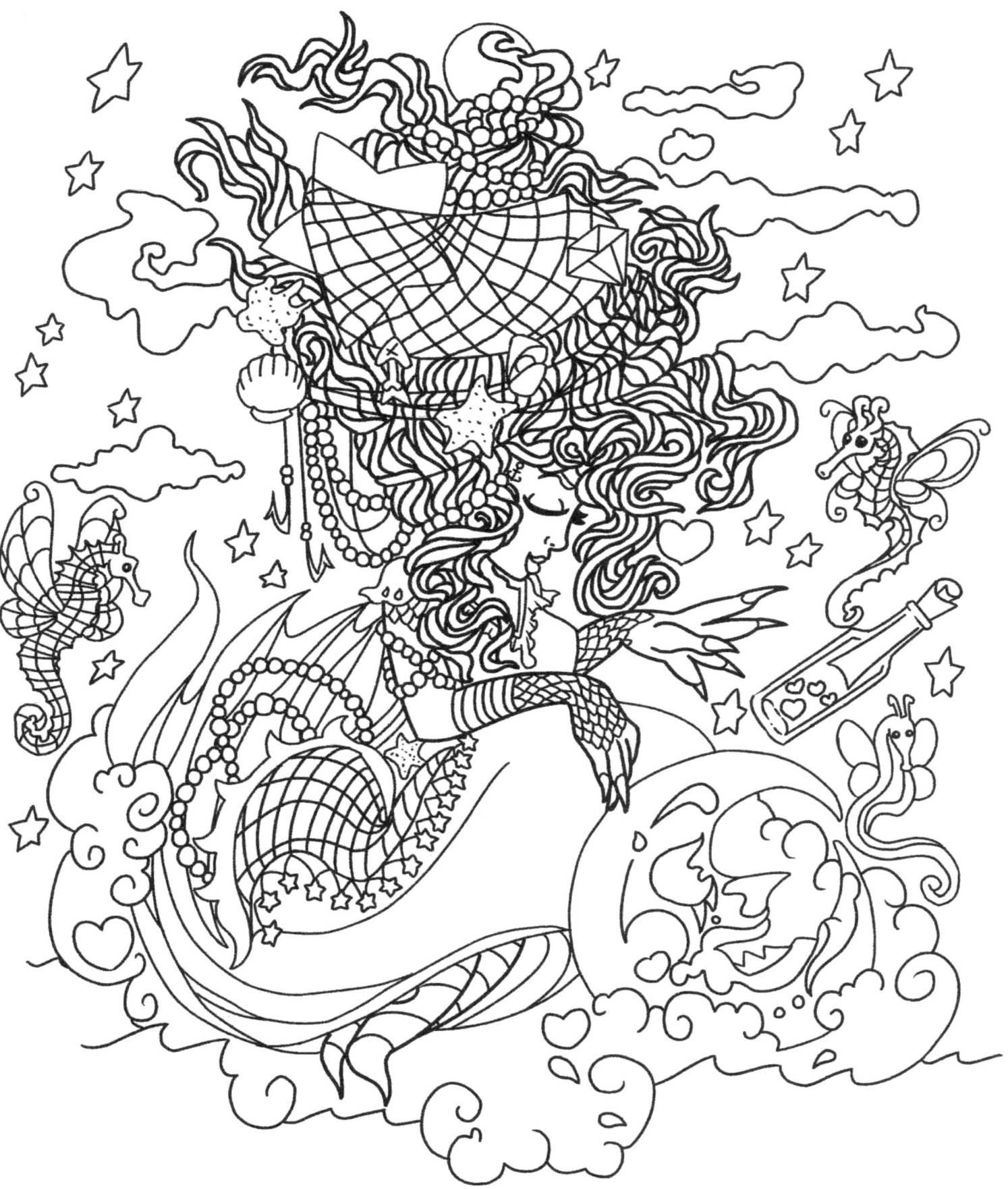

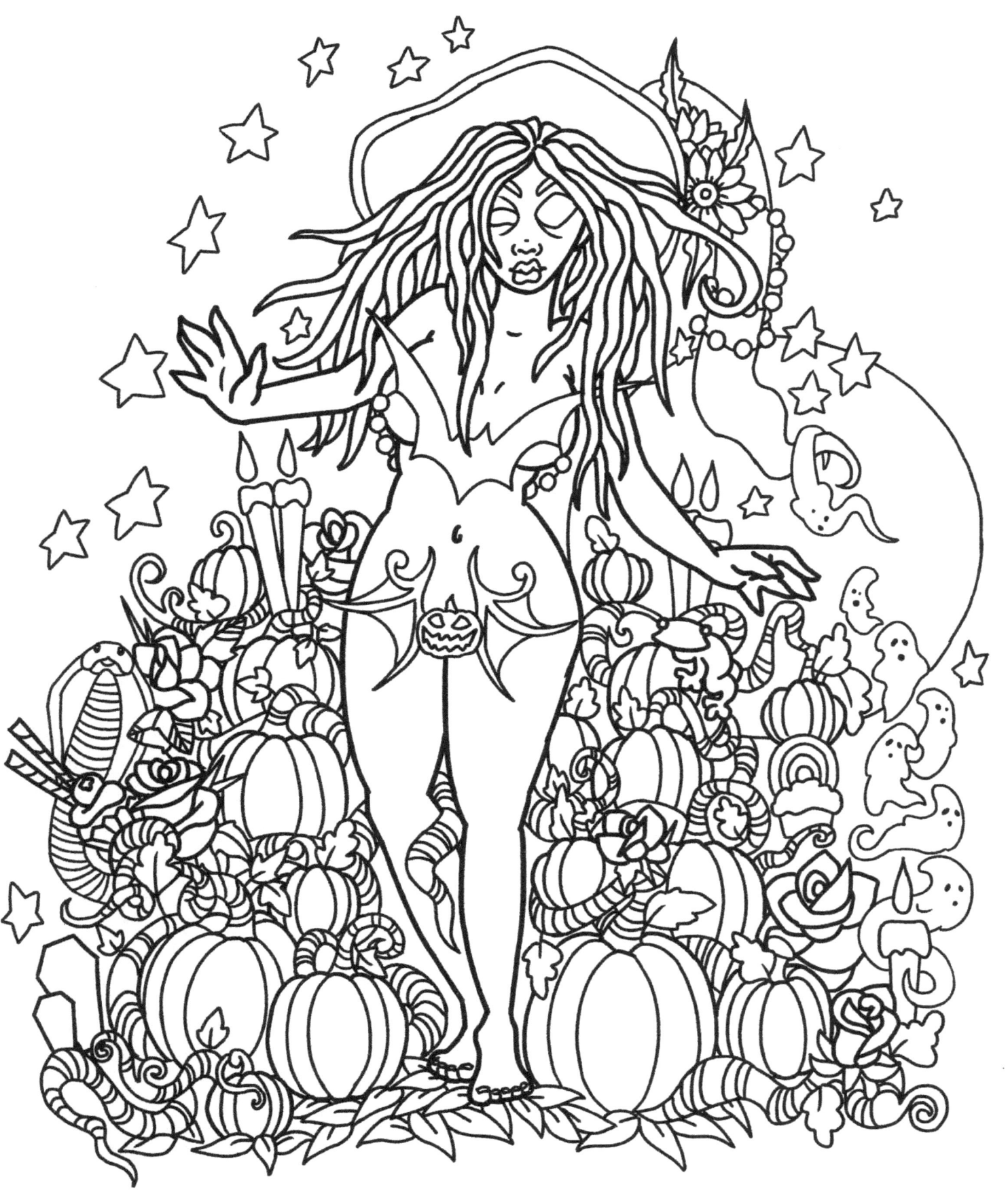

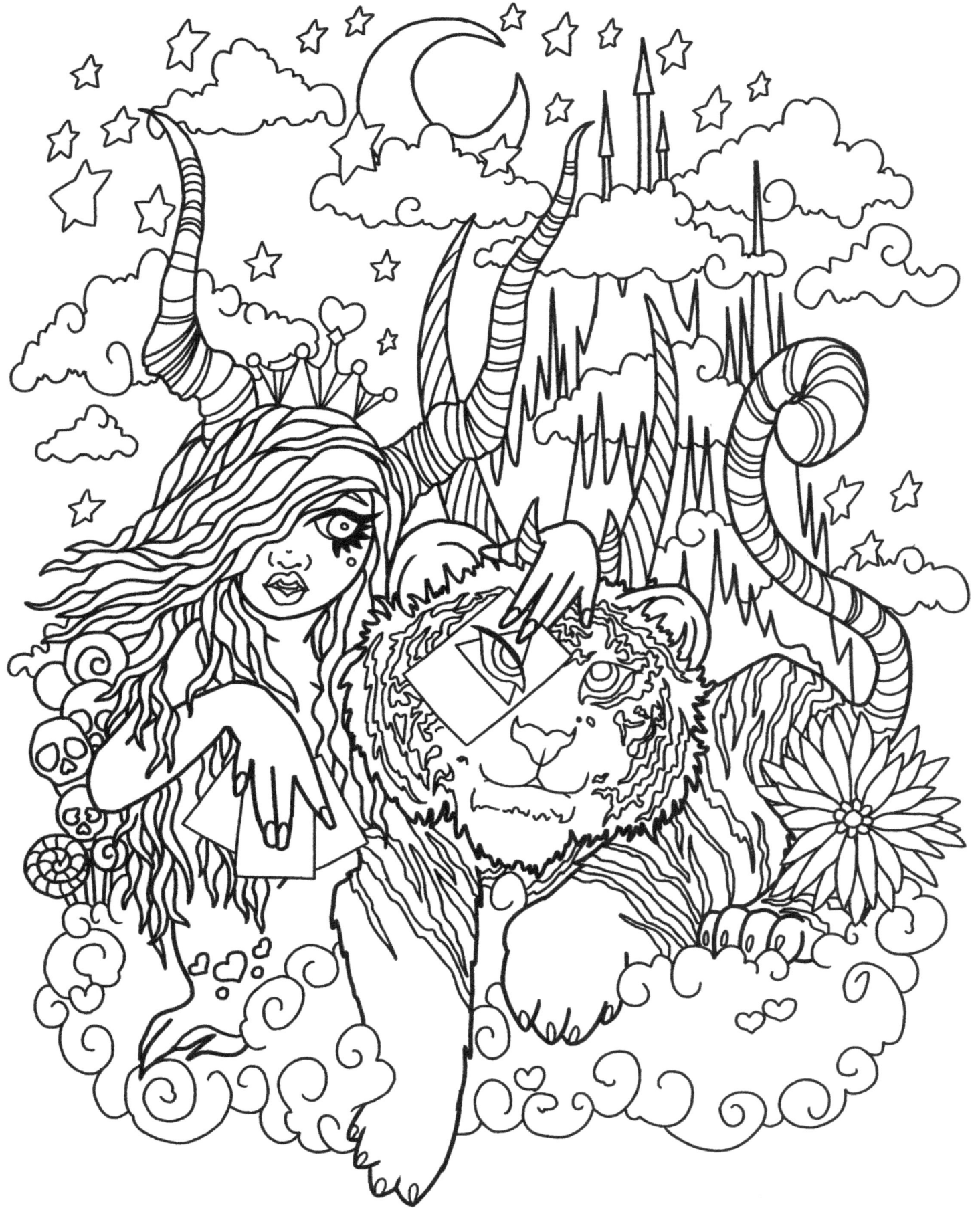

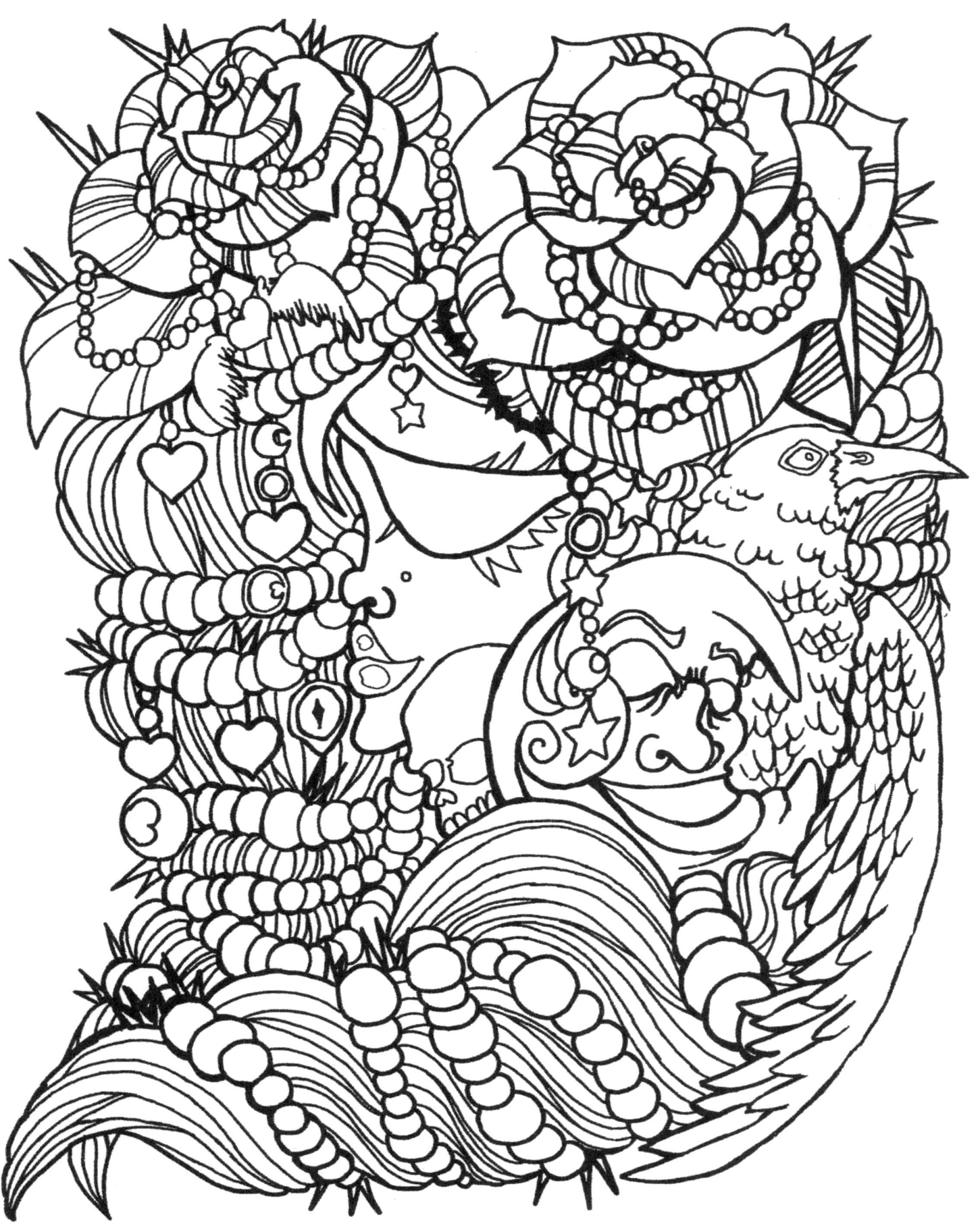

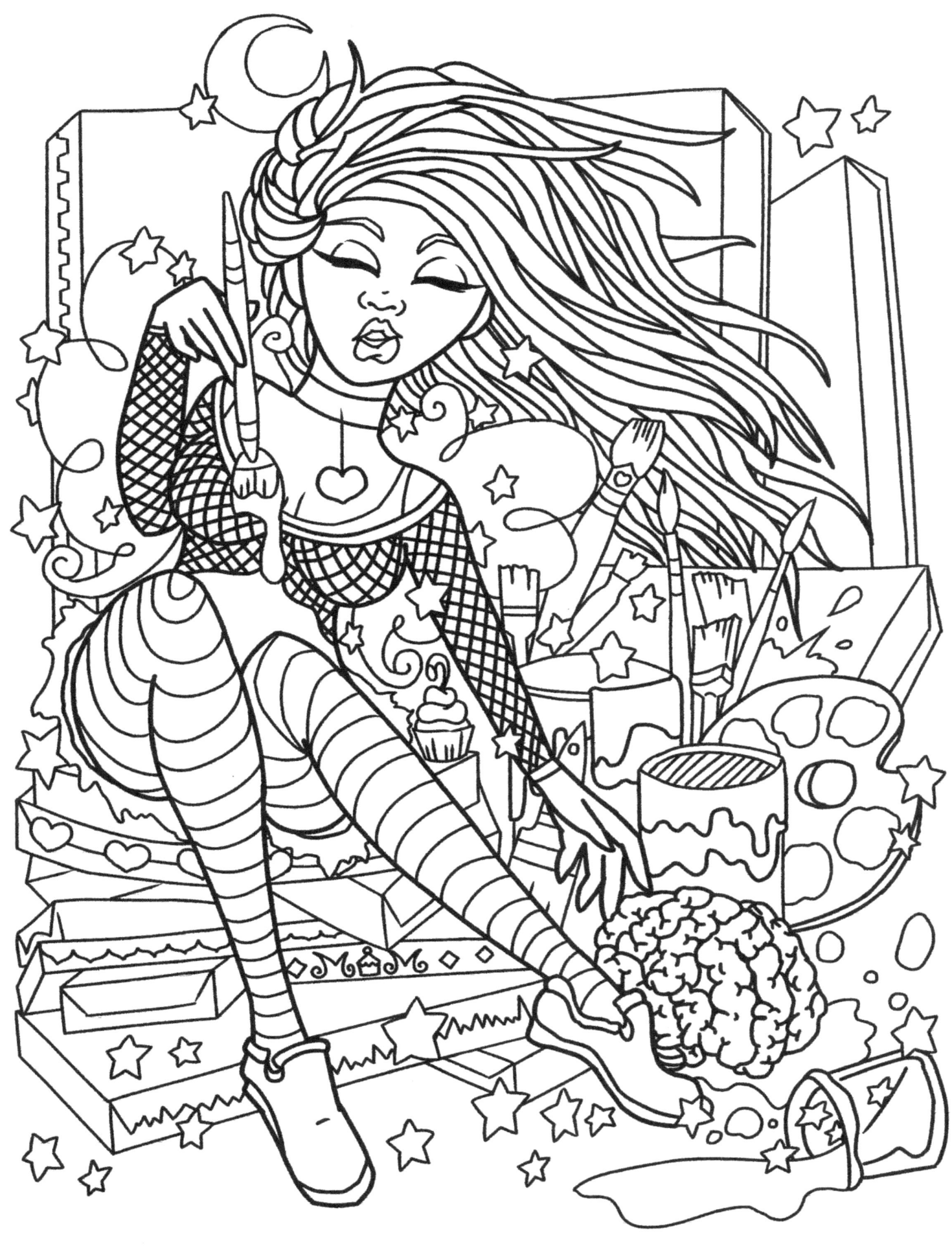

Ms. Muffintop's

Color Test Page!!!

Test your colors here!

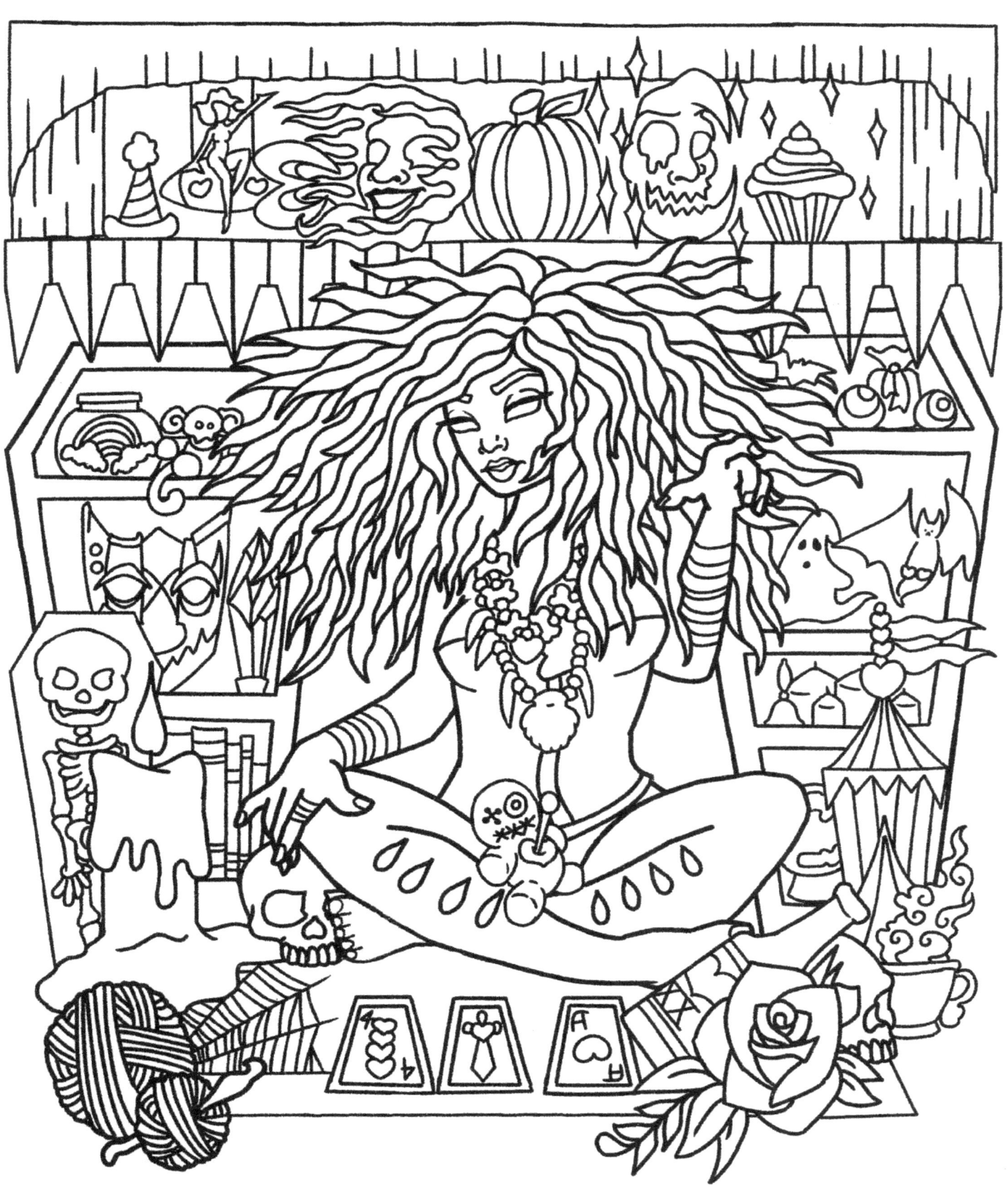

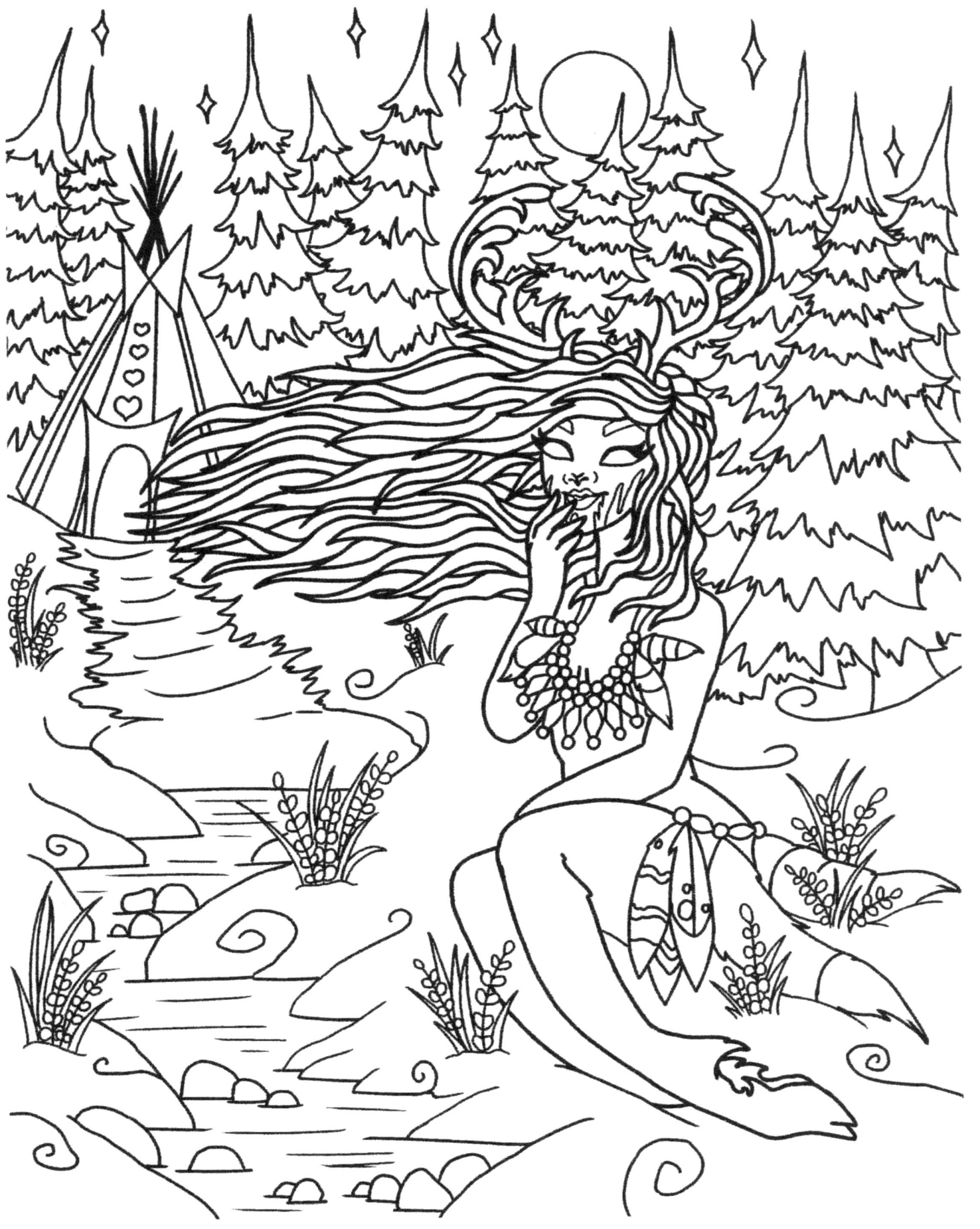

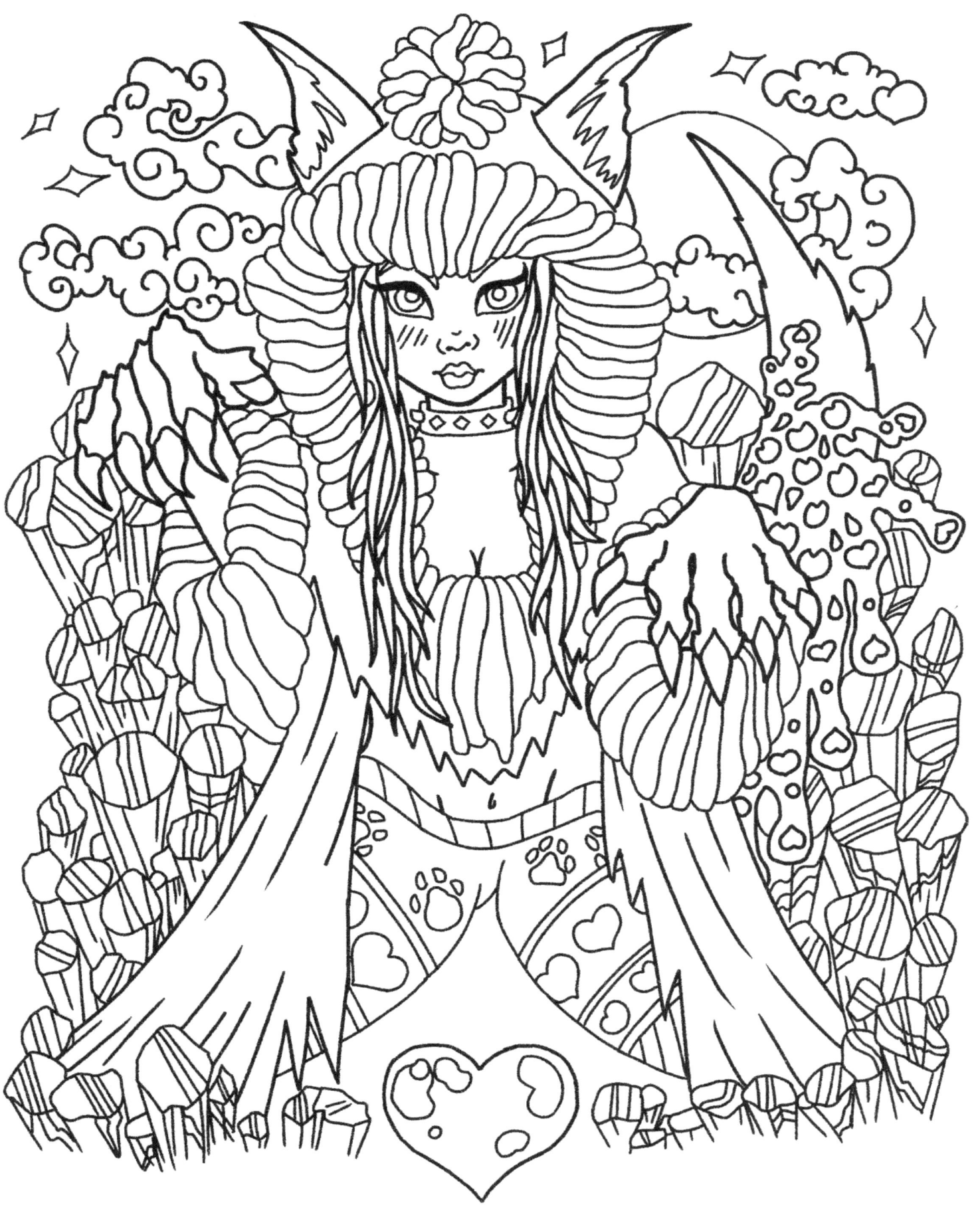

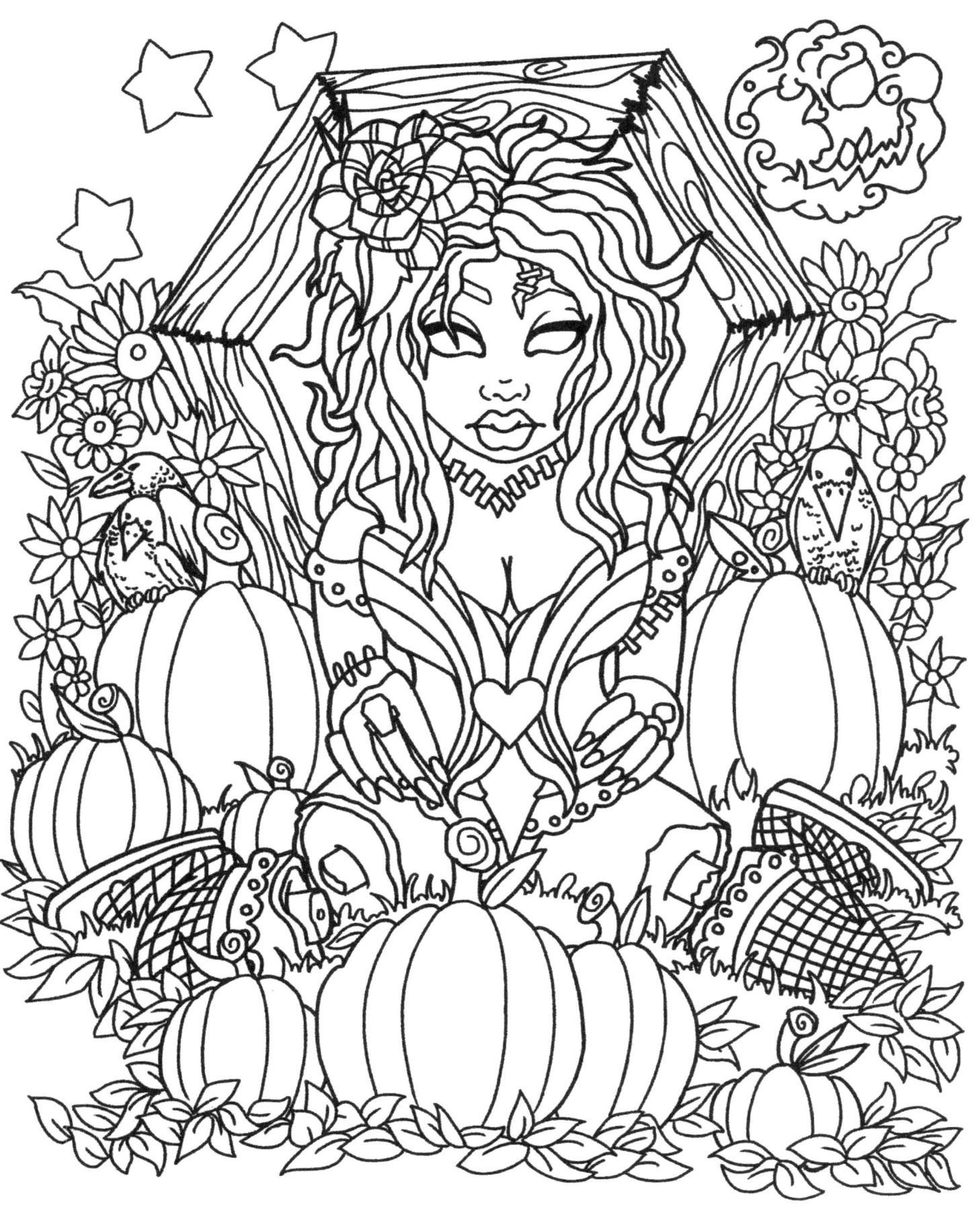

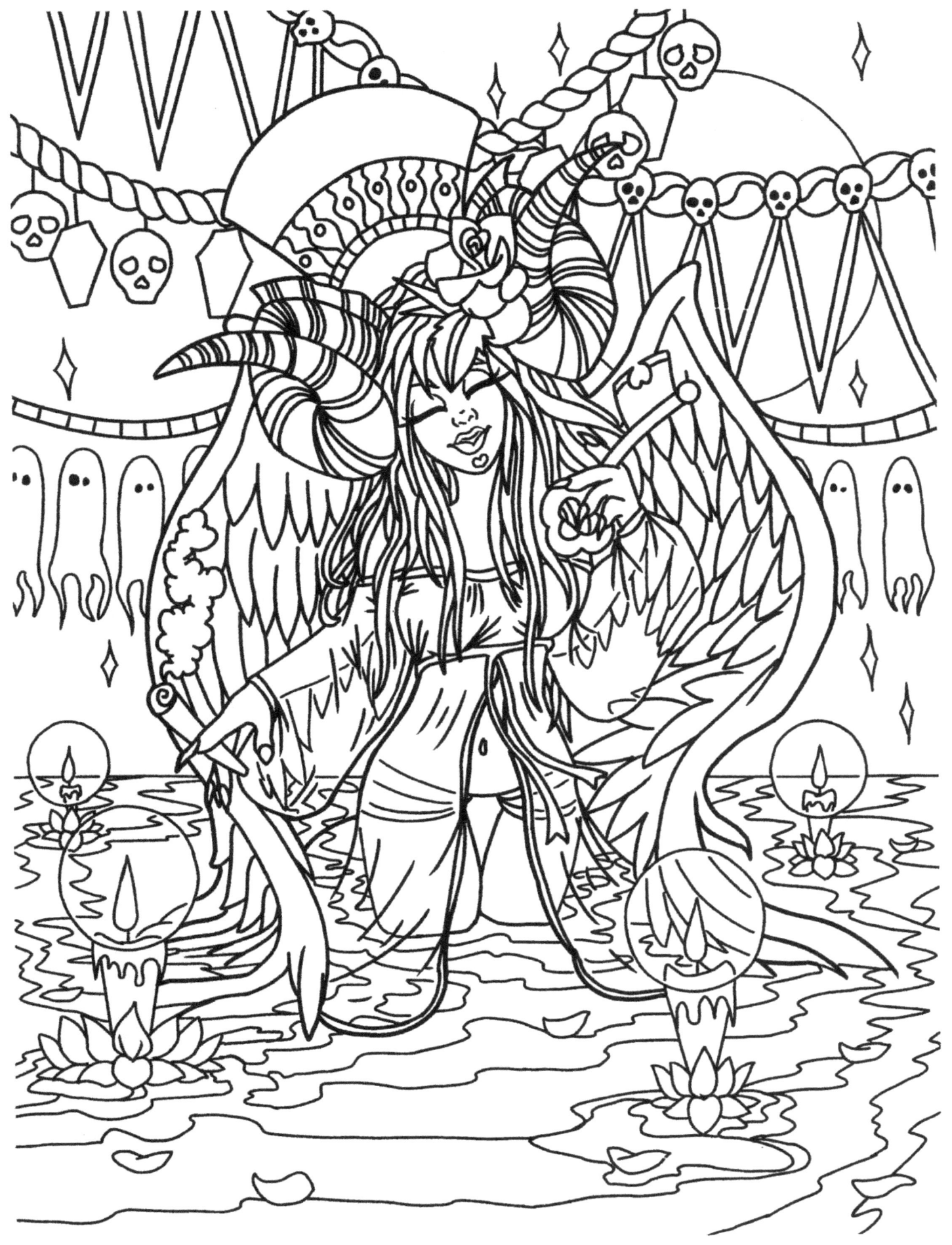

Ms. Muffintop's

Color Test Page!!!

Test your colors here!

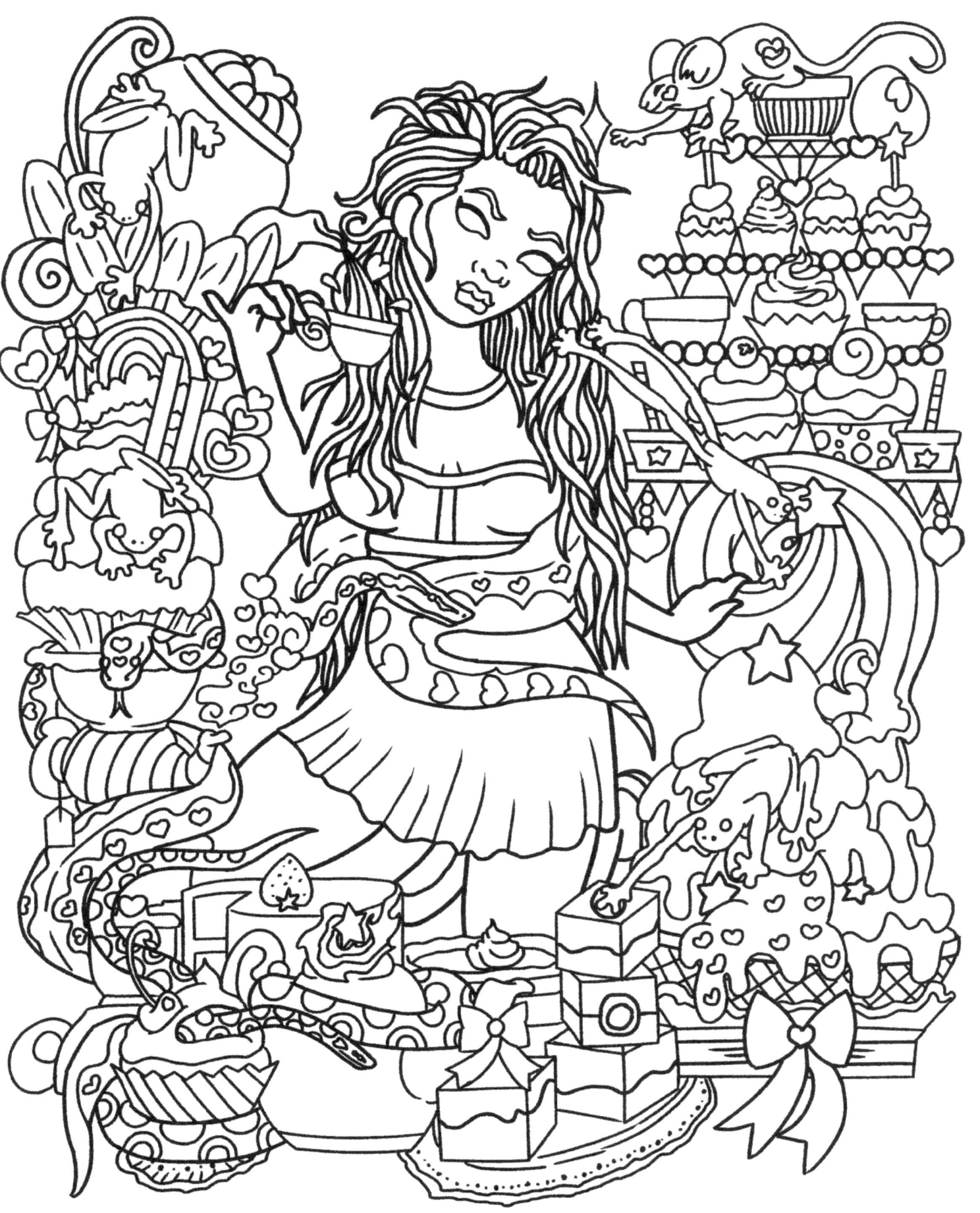

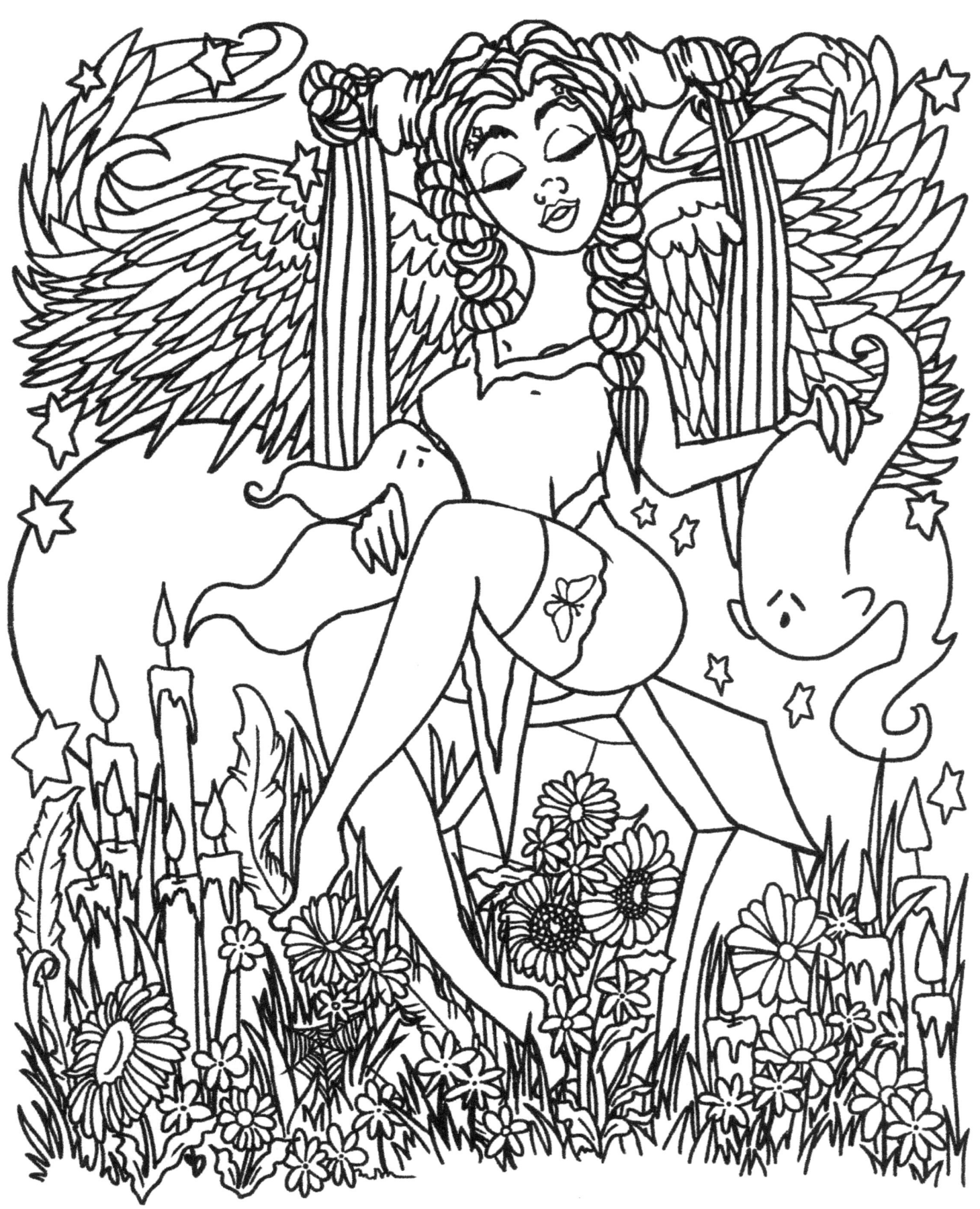

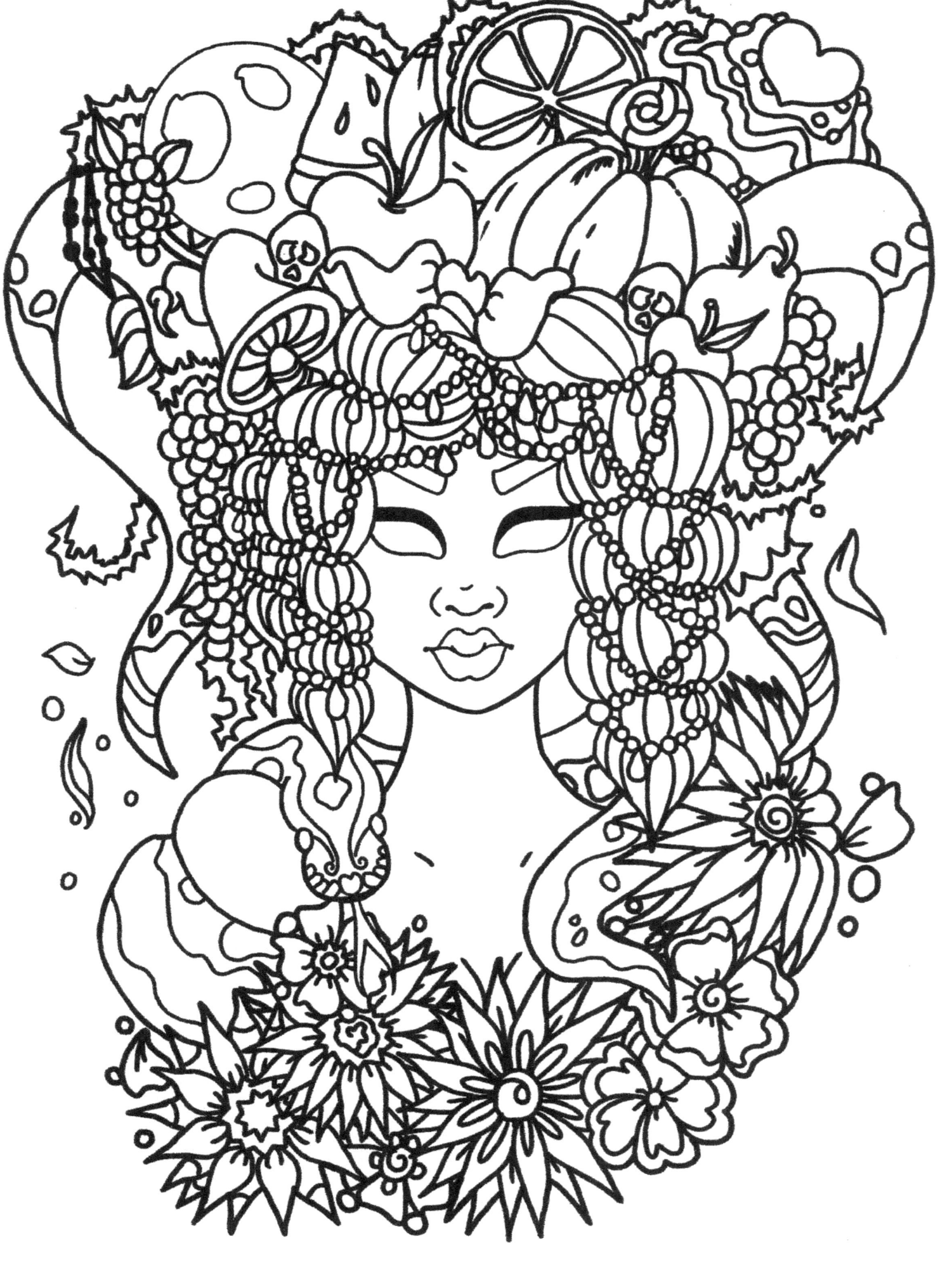

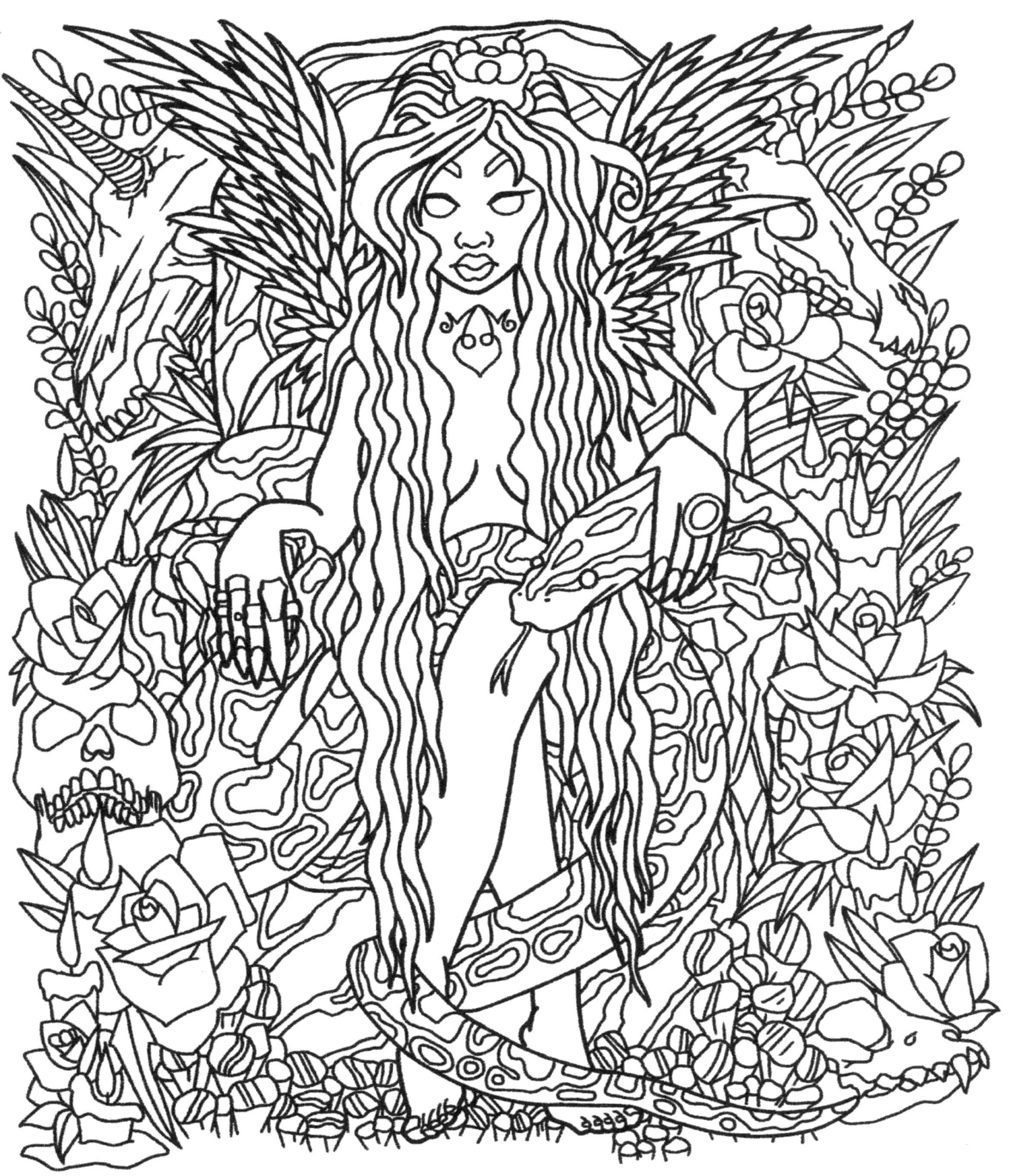

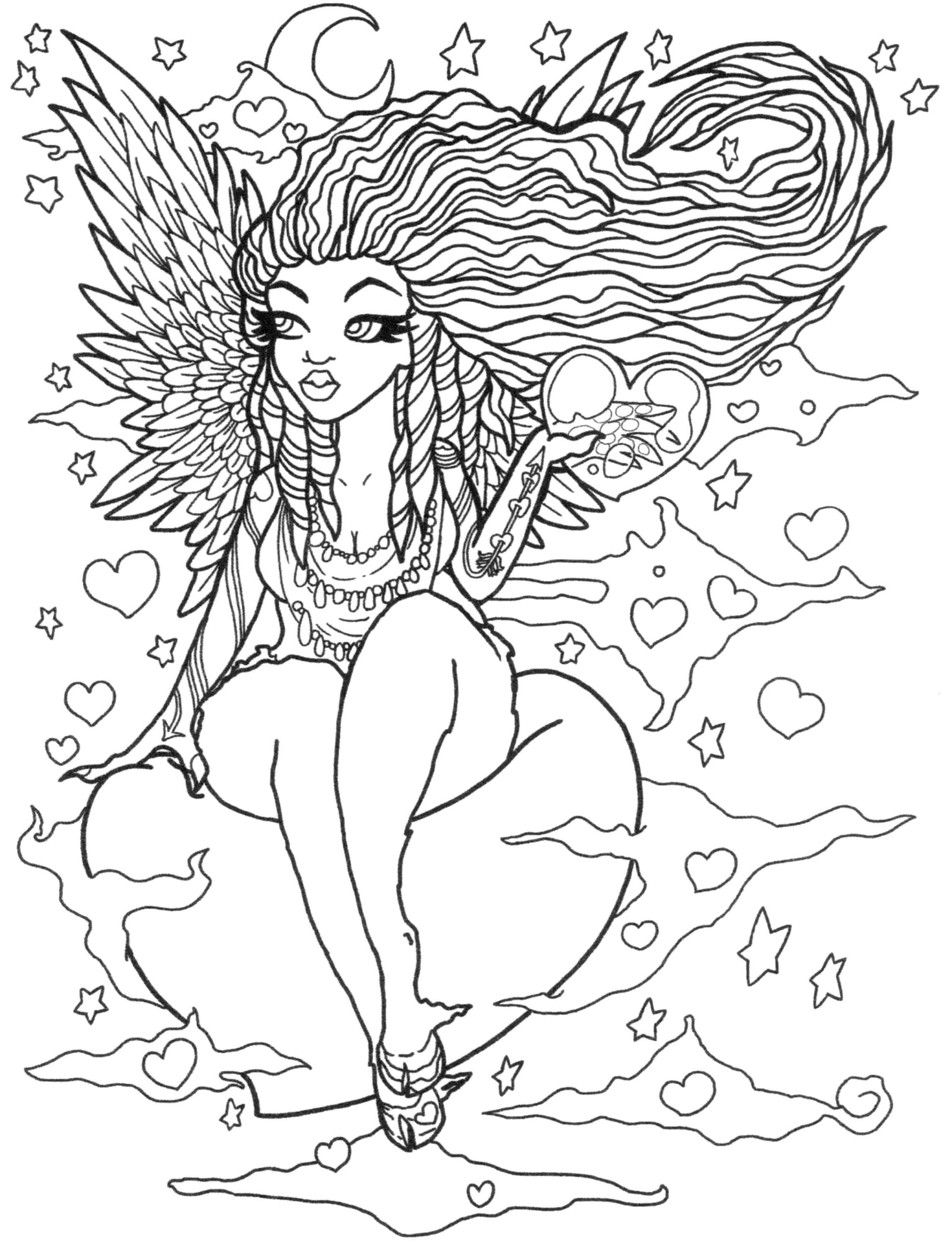

Ms. Muffintop's

Color Test Page!!!

Test your colors here!

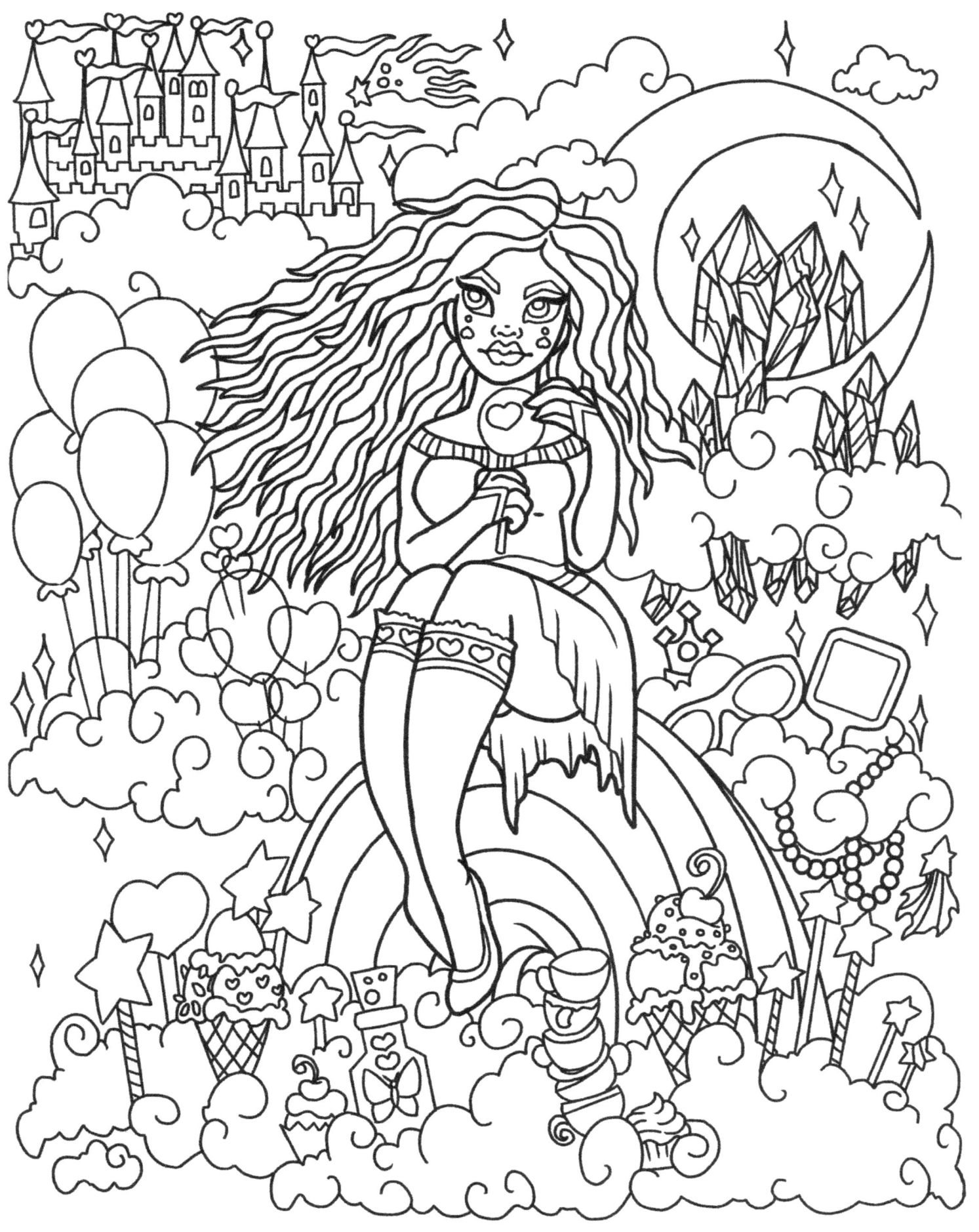

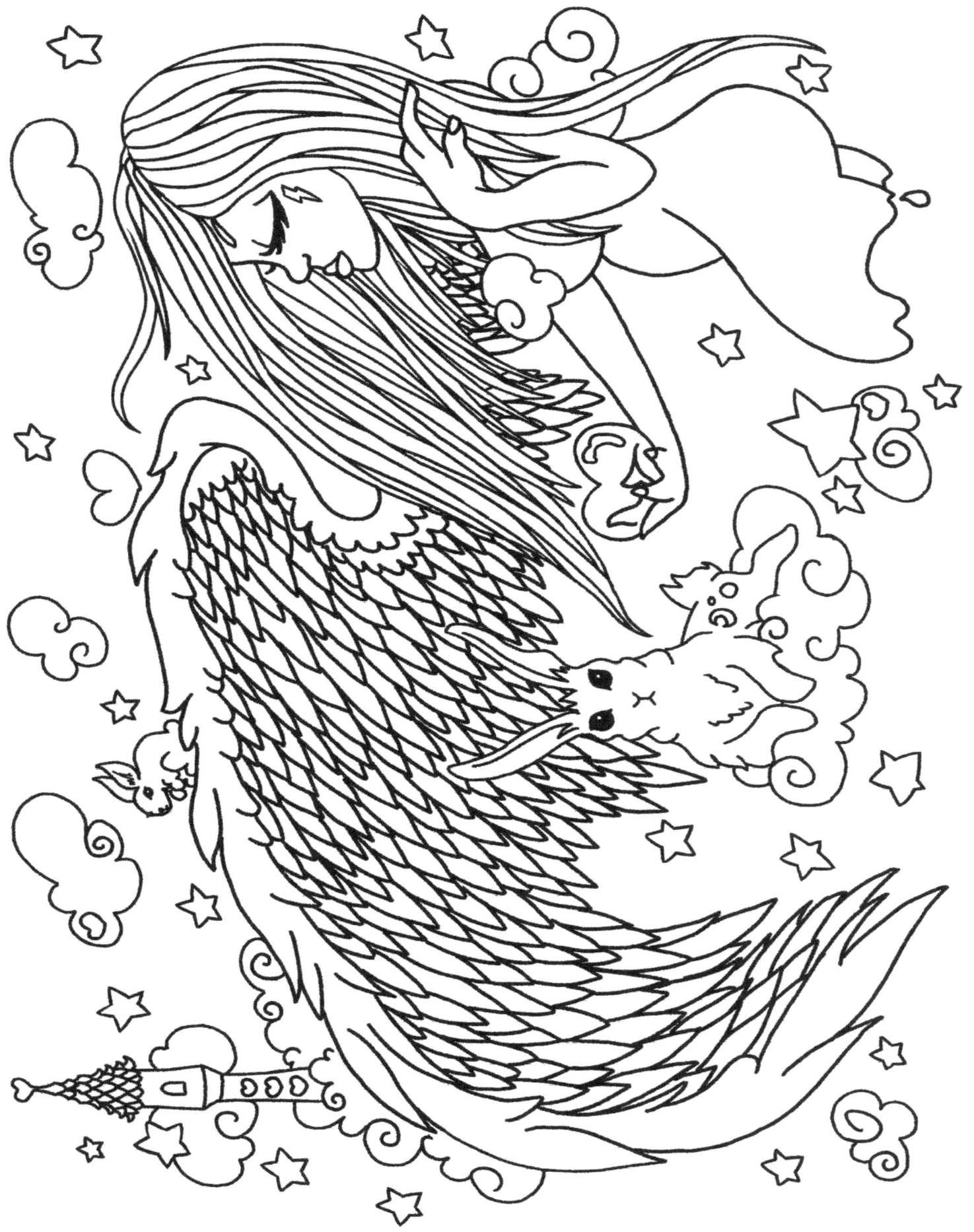

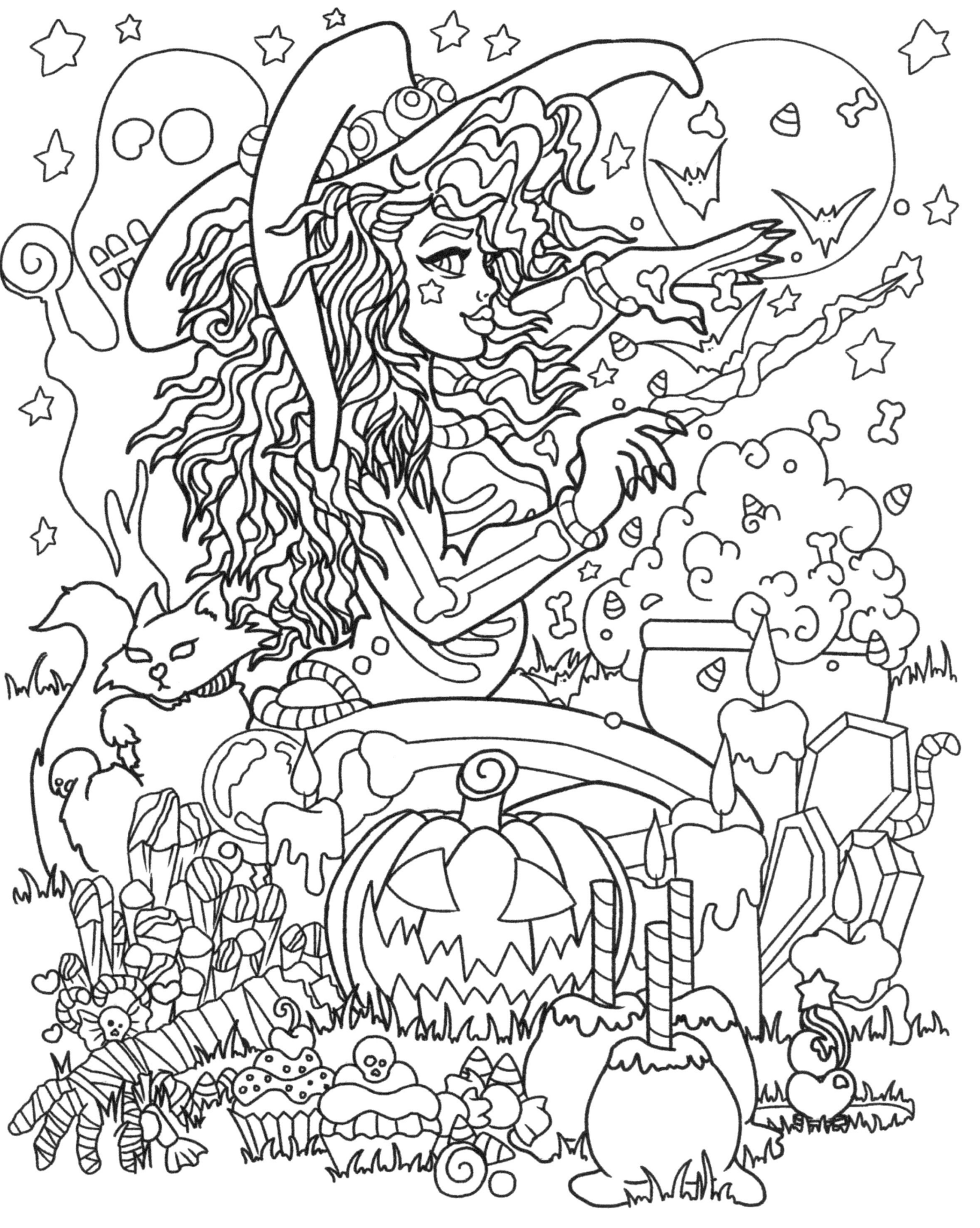

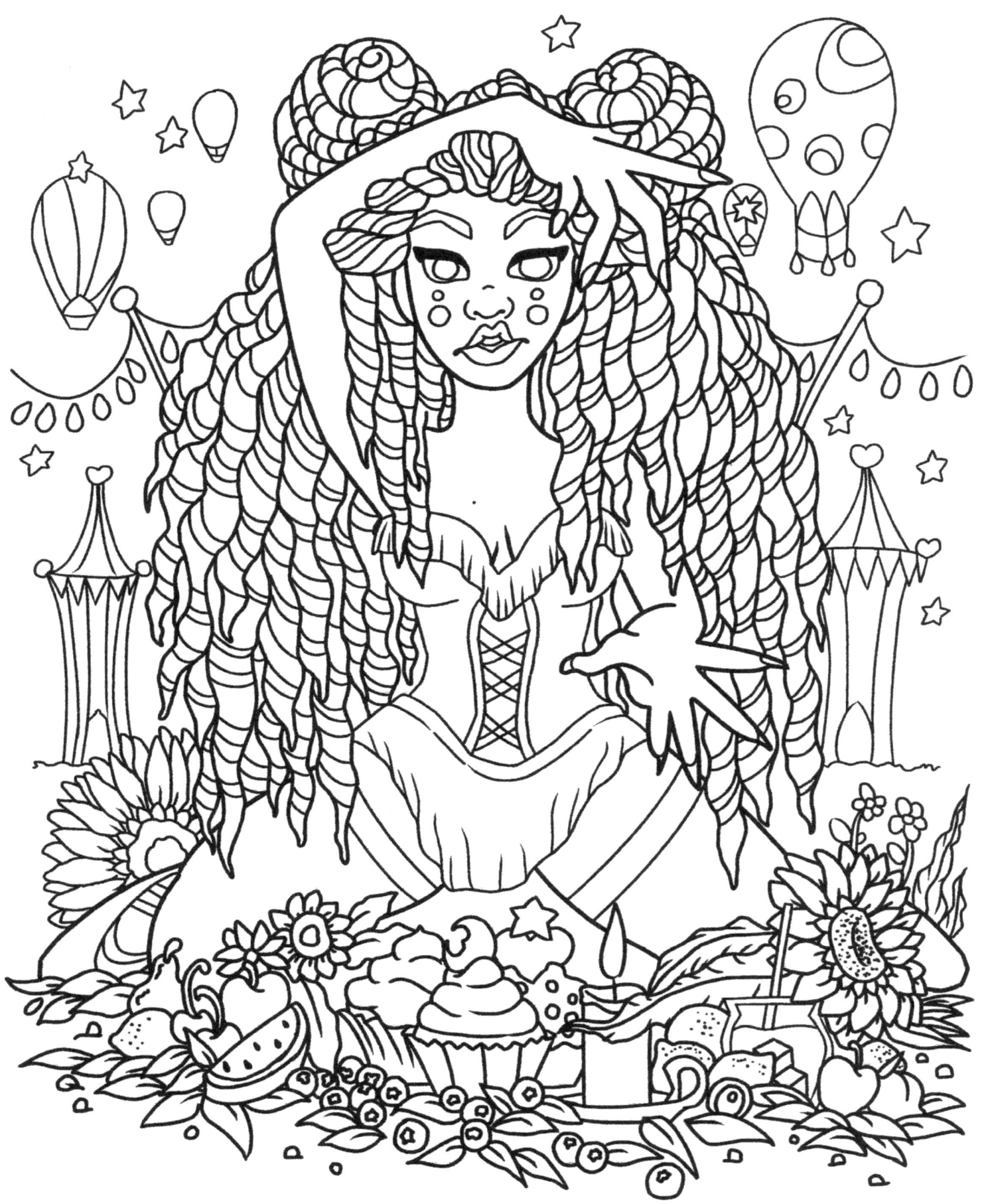

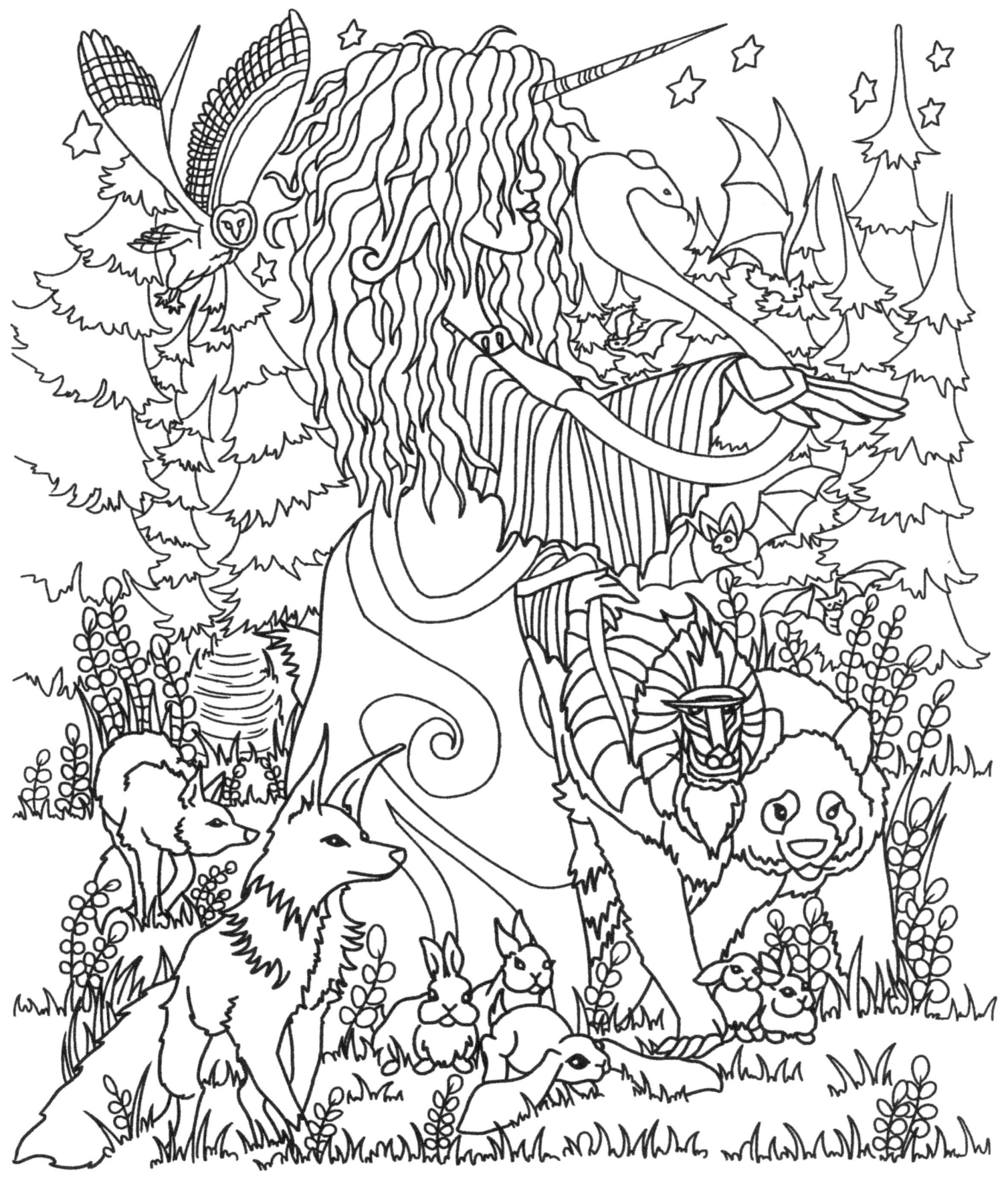

Ms. Muffintop's

Color Test Page!!!

Test your colors here!

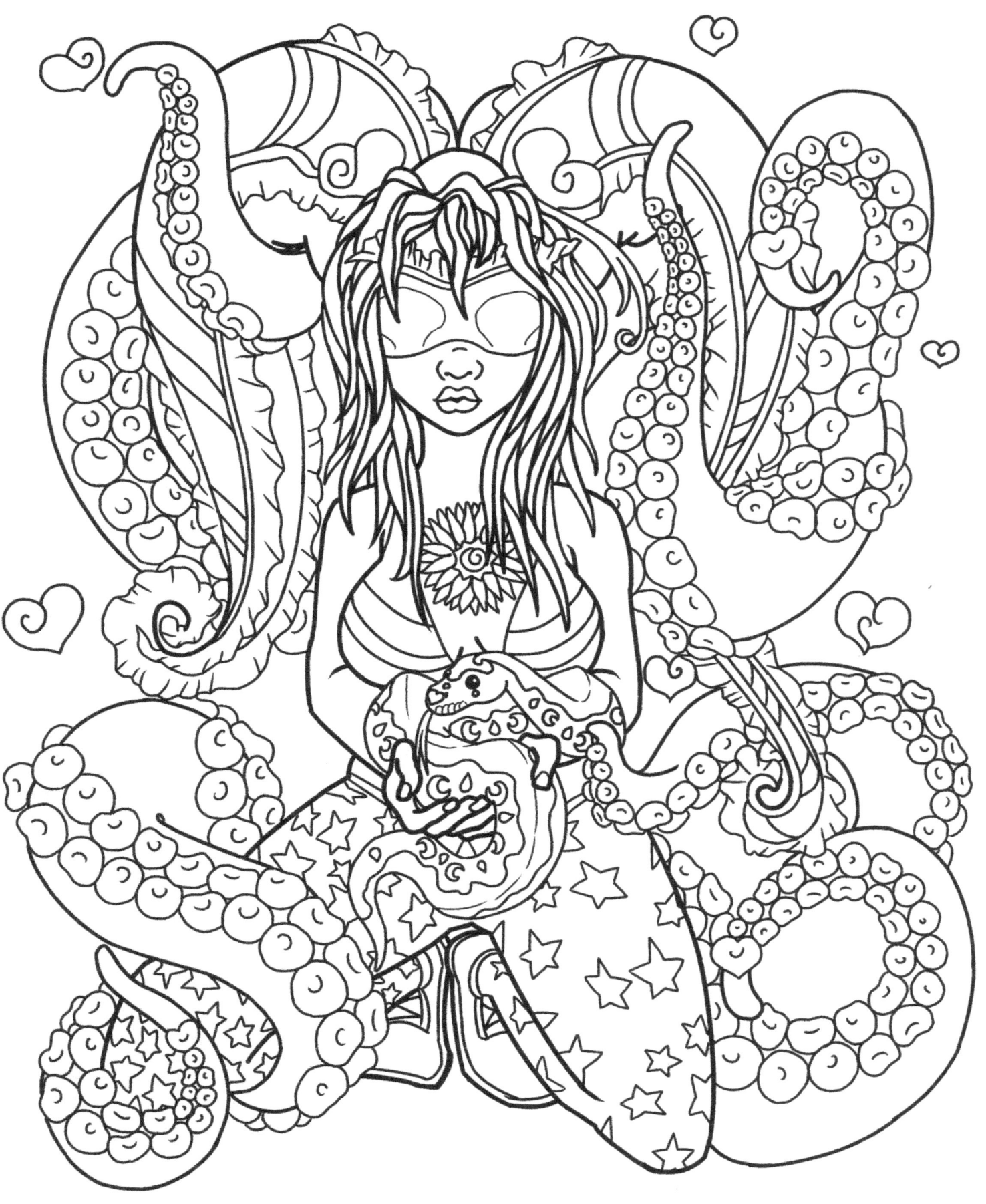

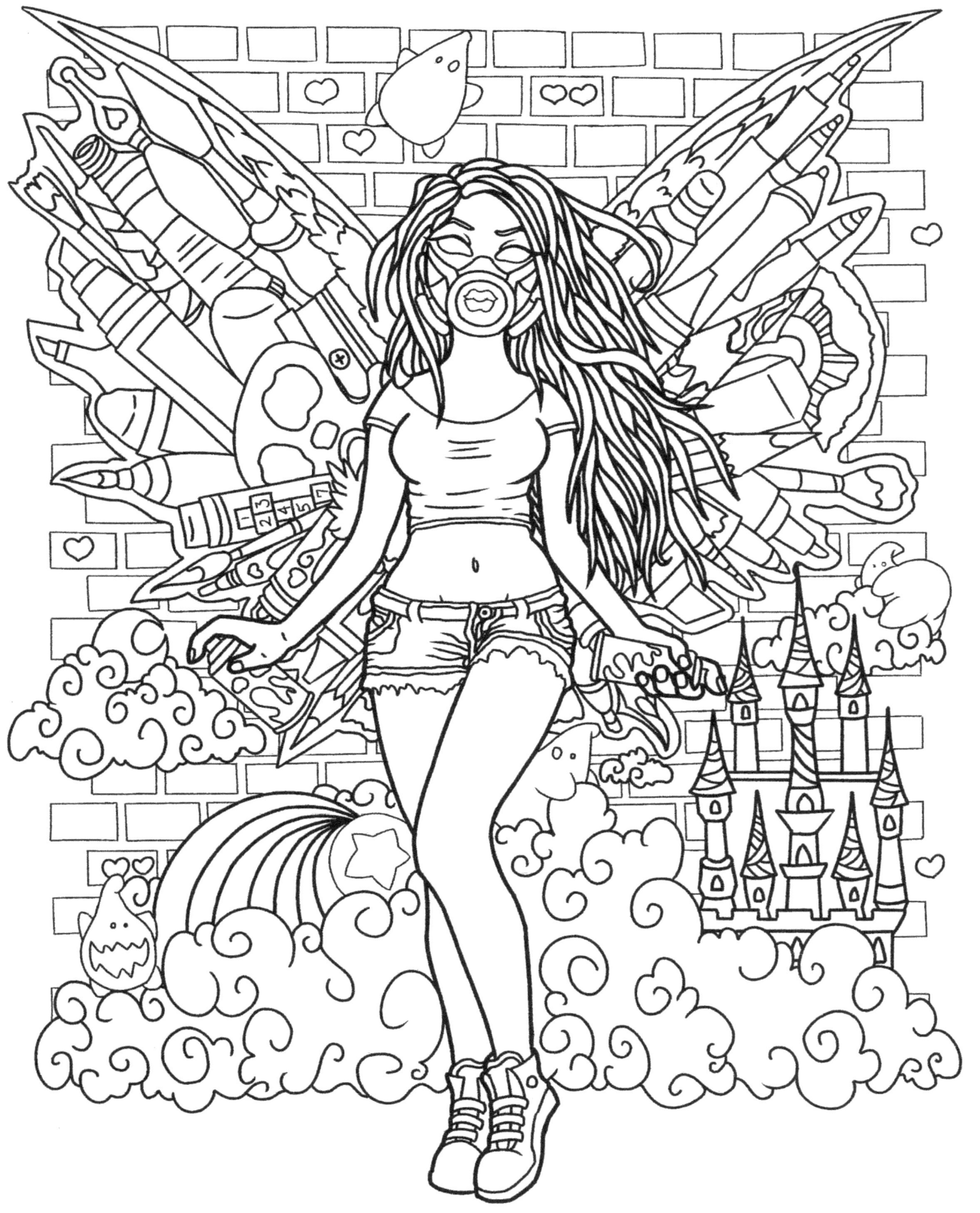

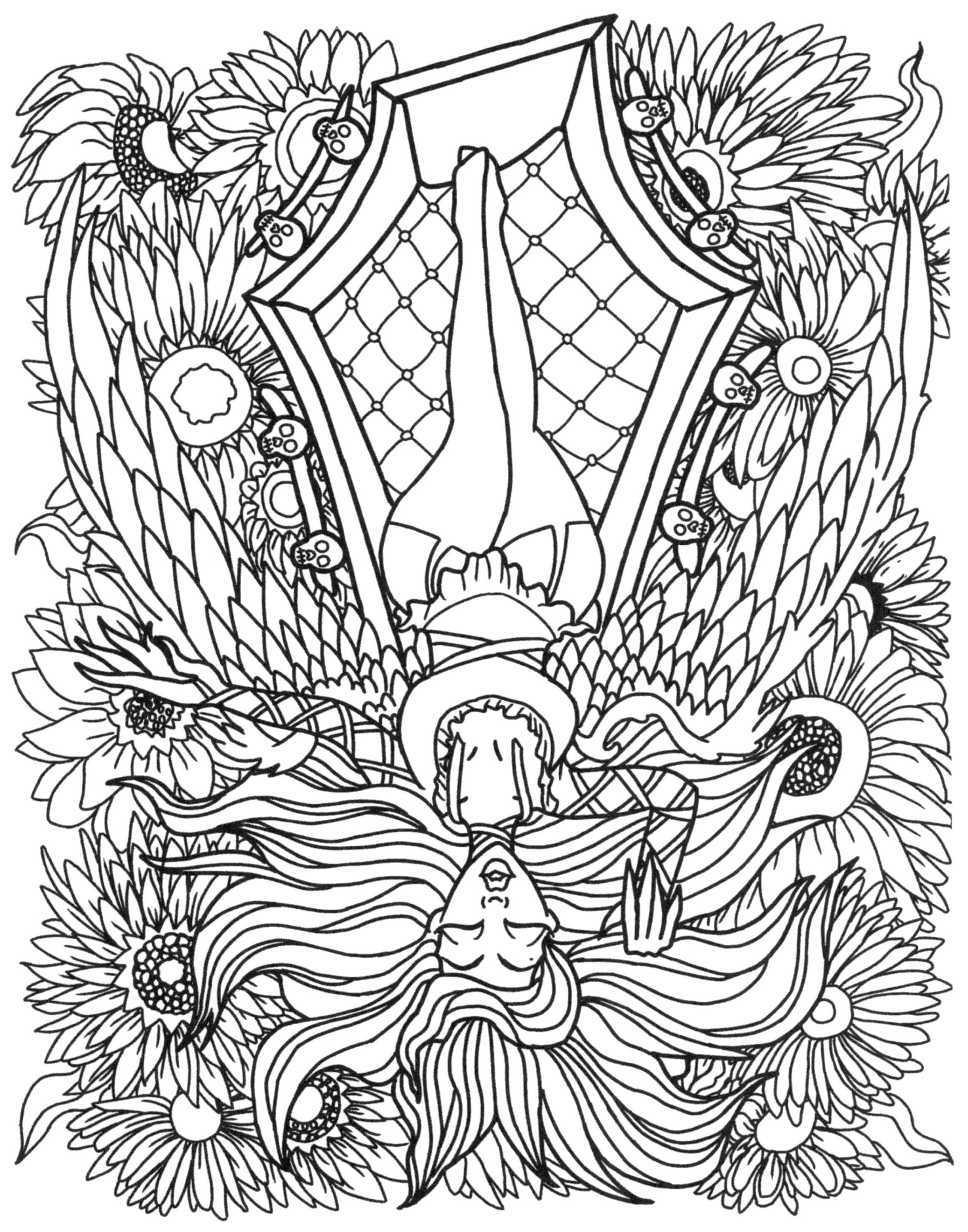

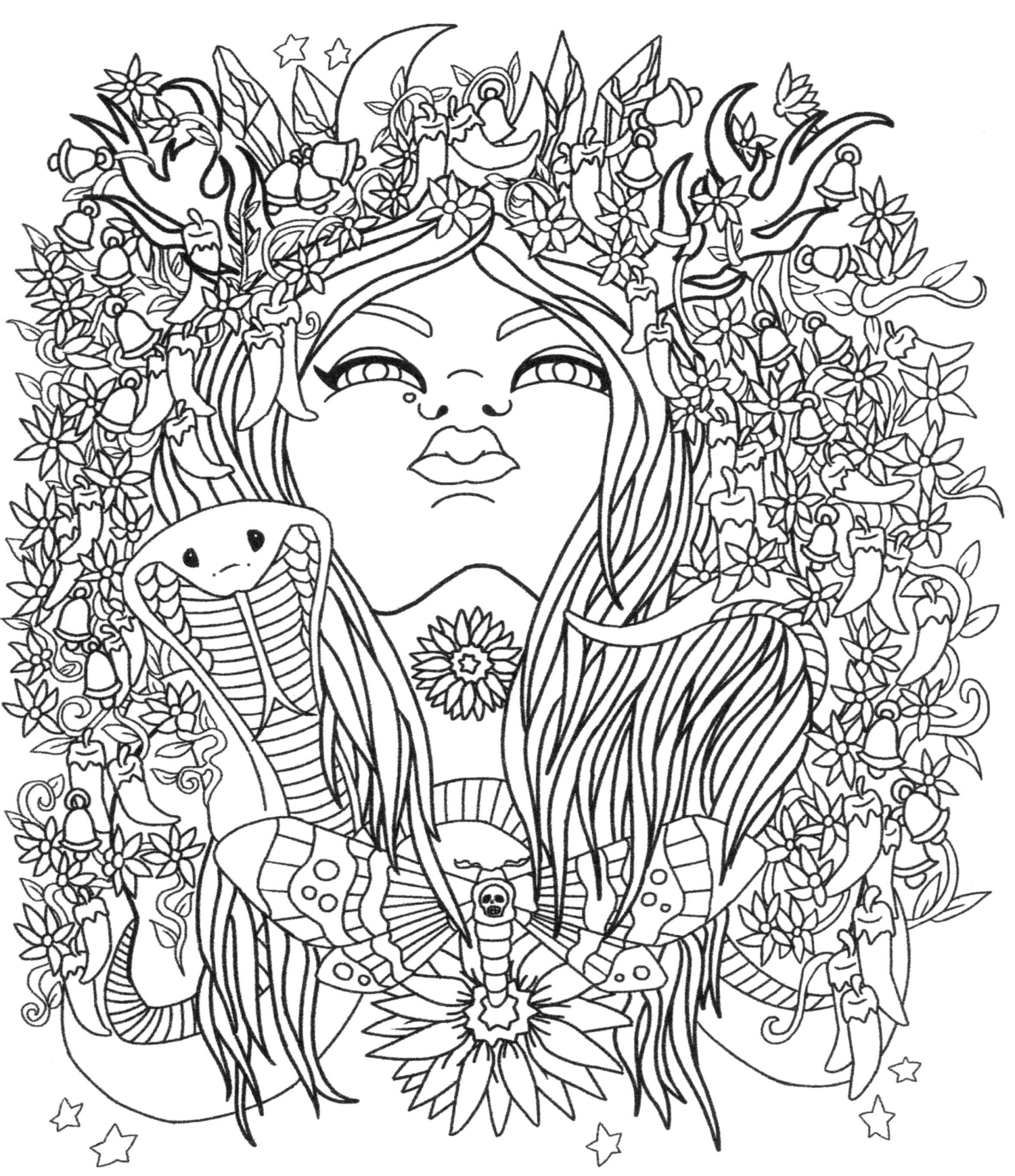

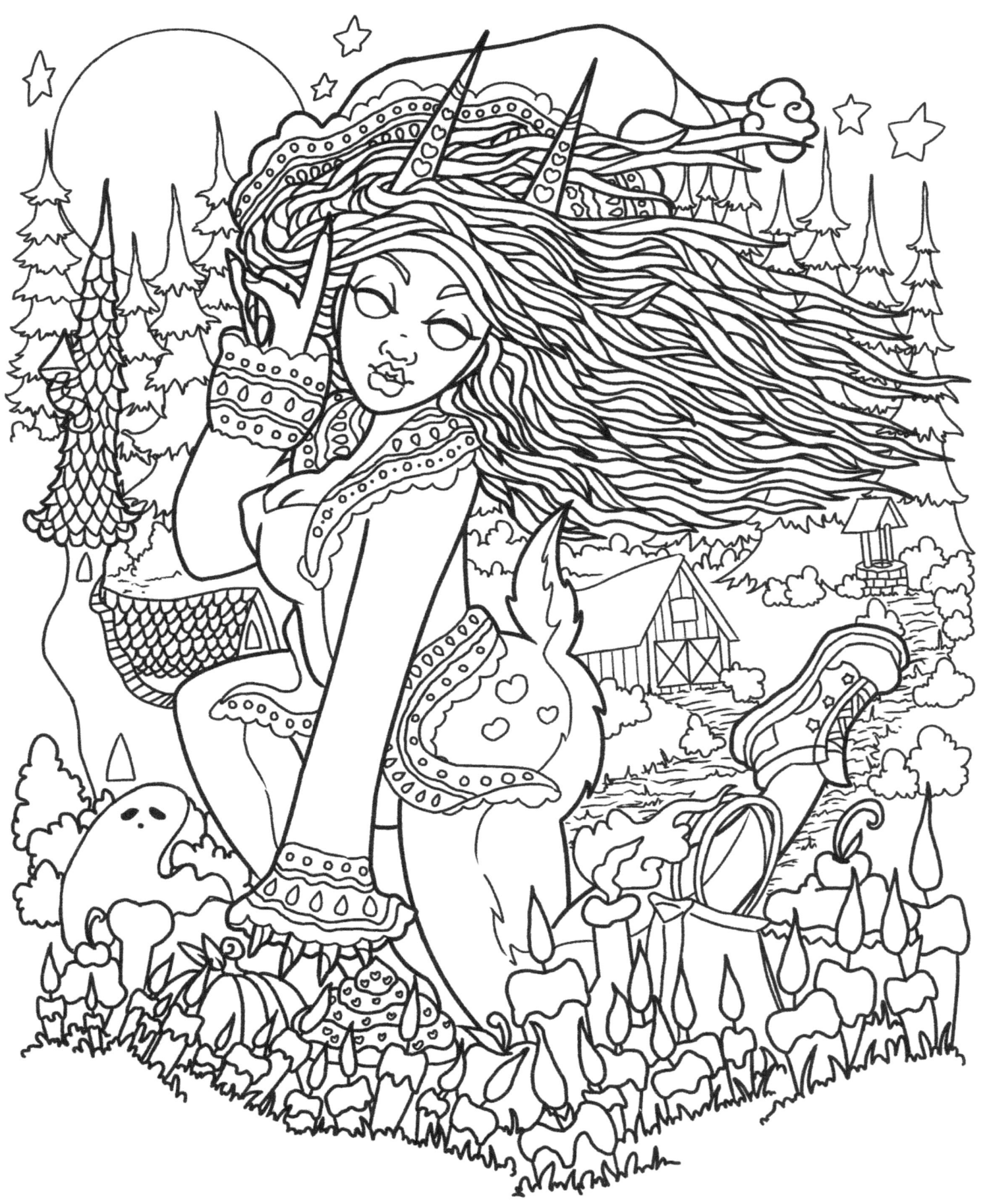

Ms. Muffintop's

Color Test Page!!!

Test your colors here!

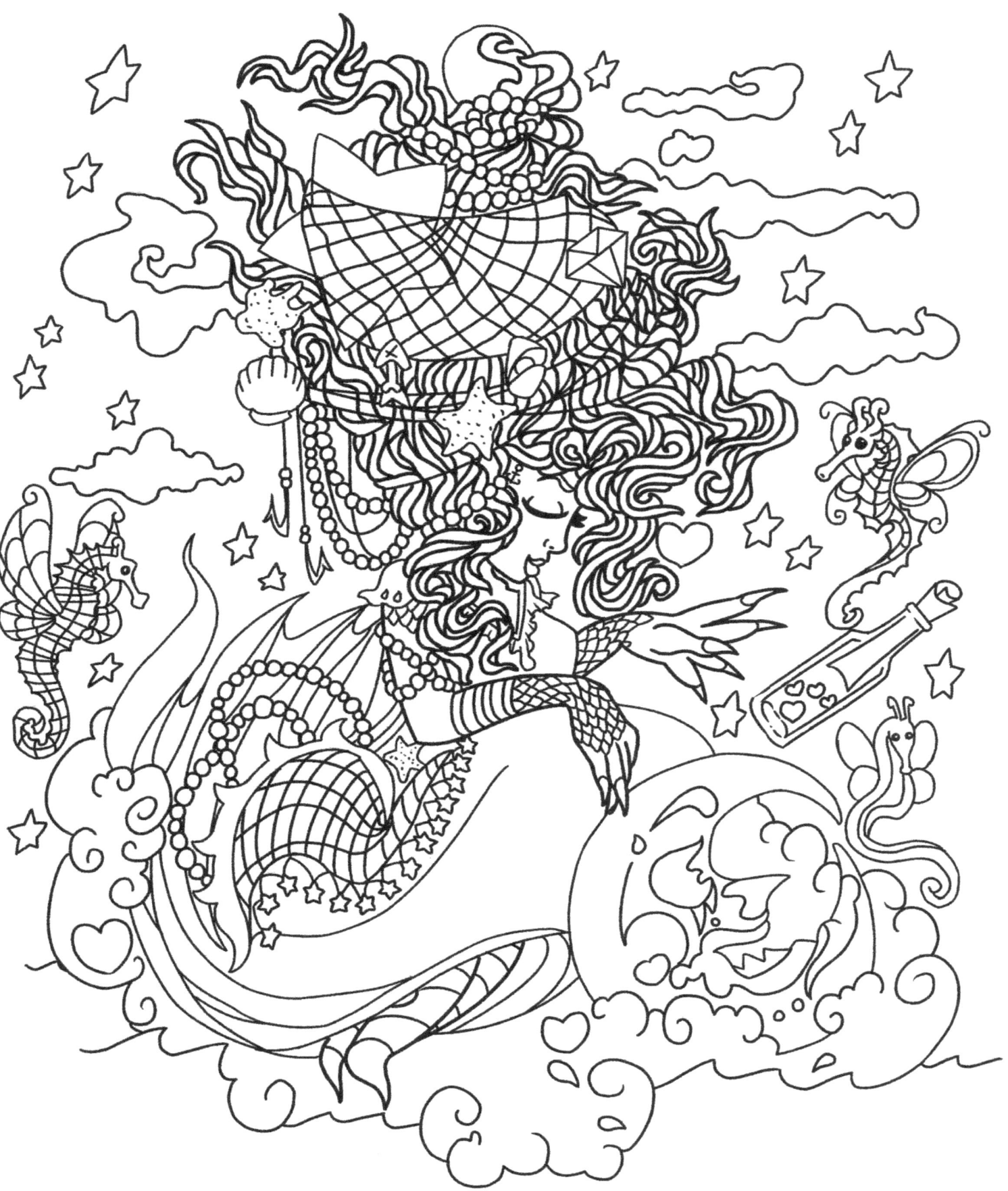

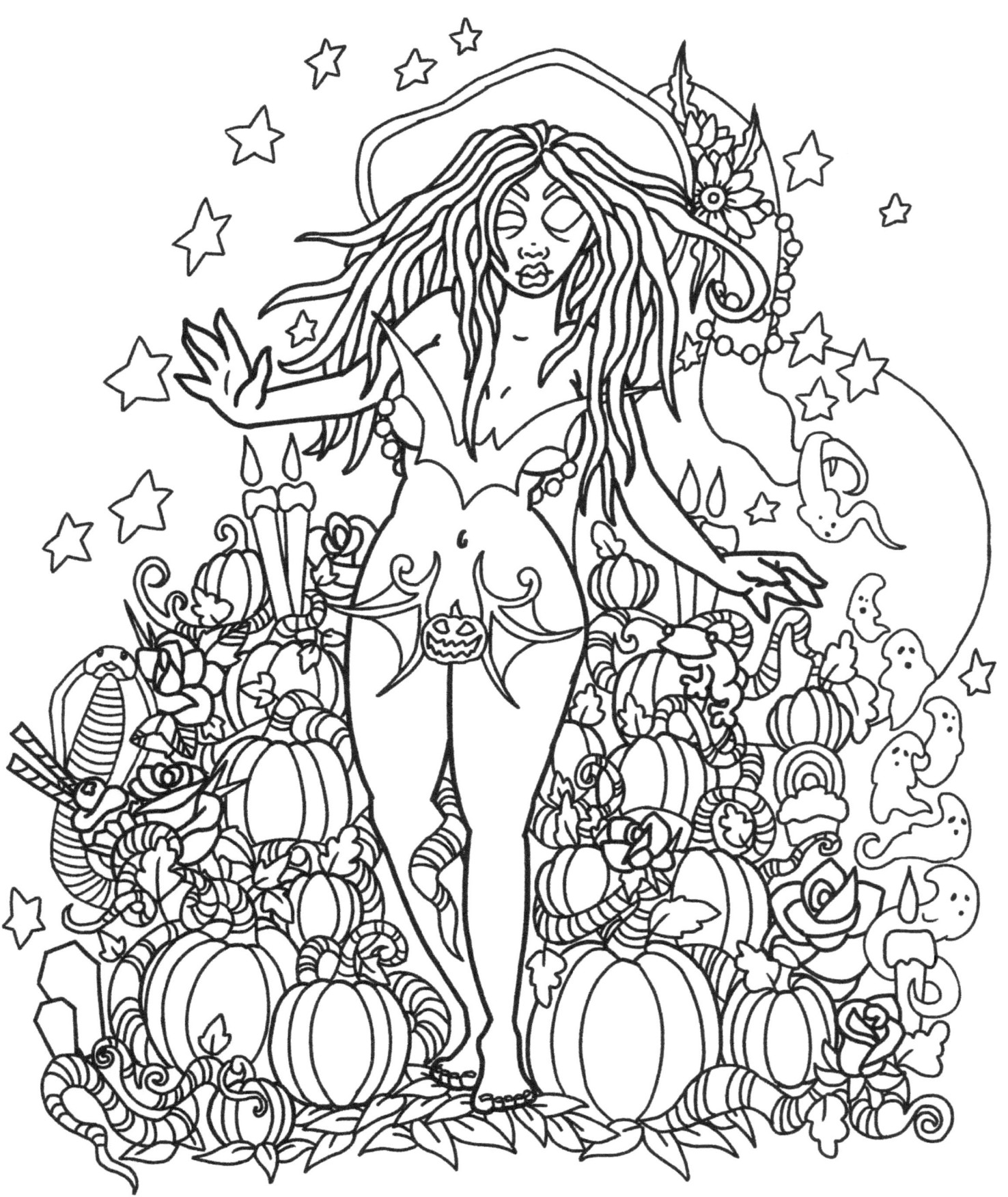

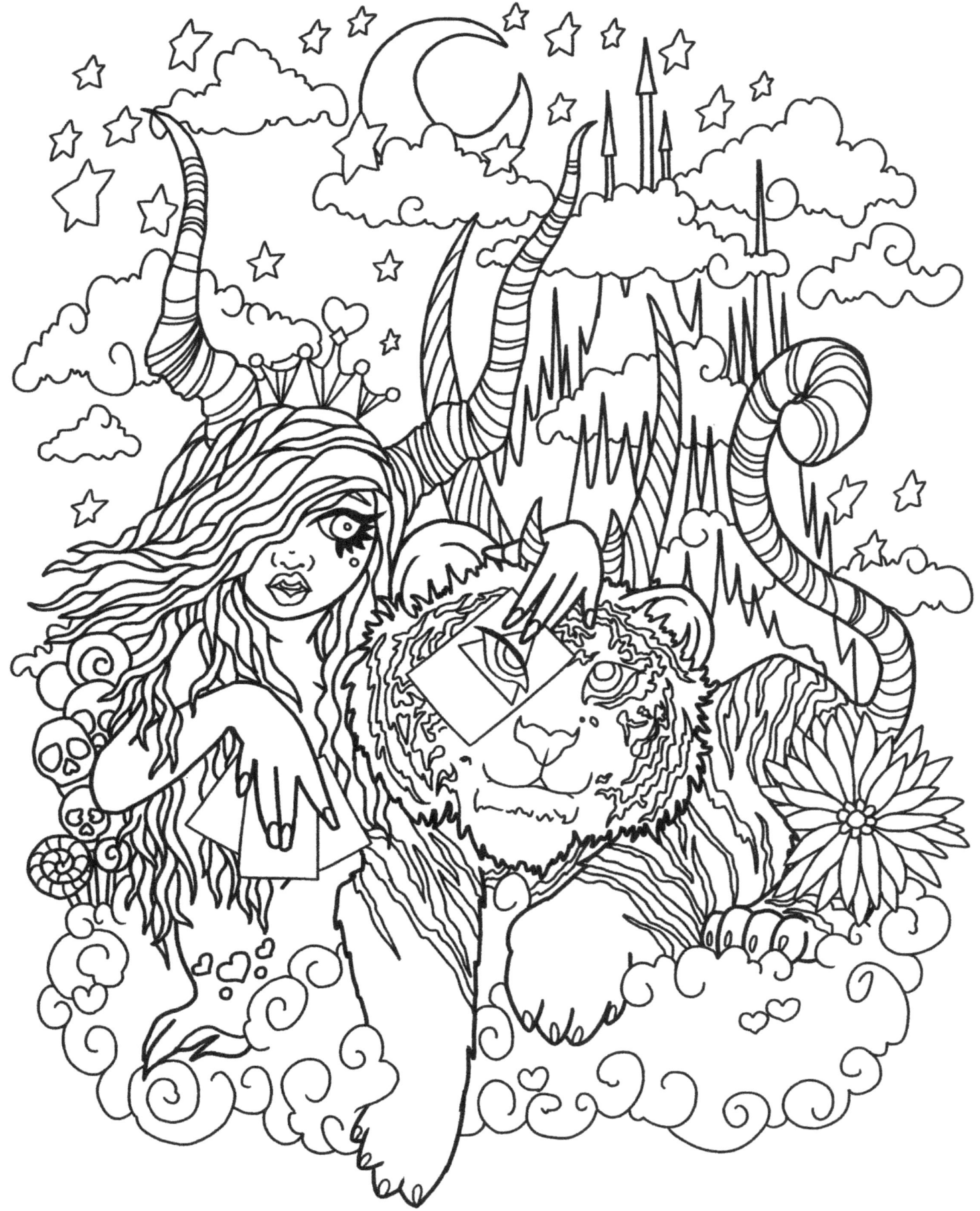

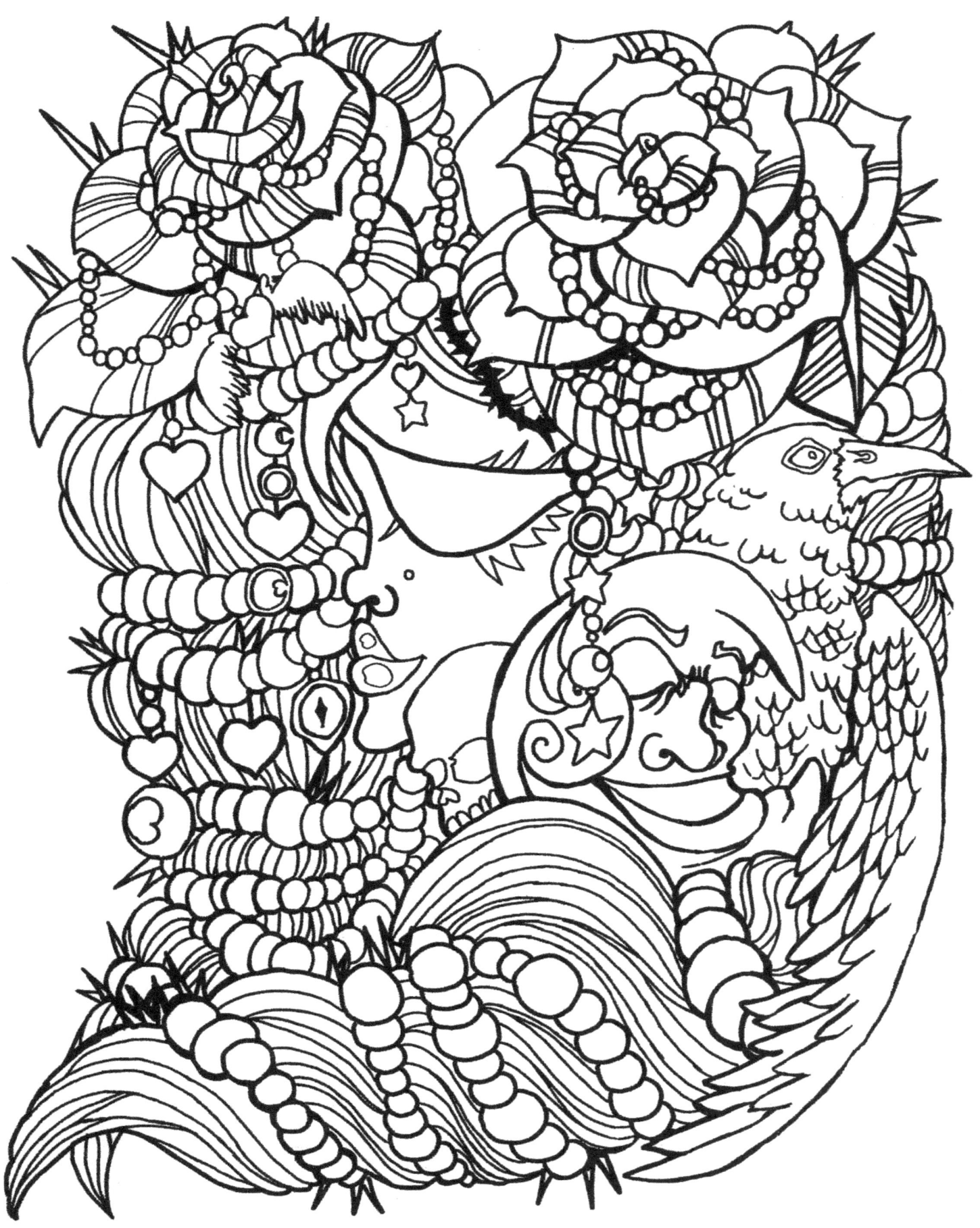

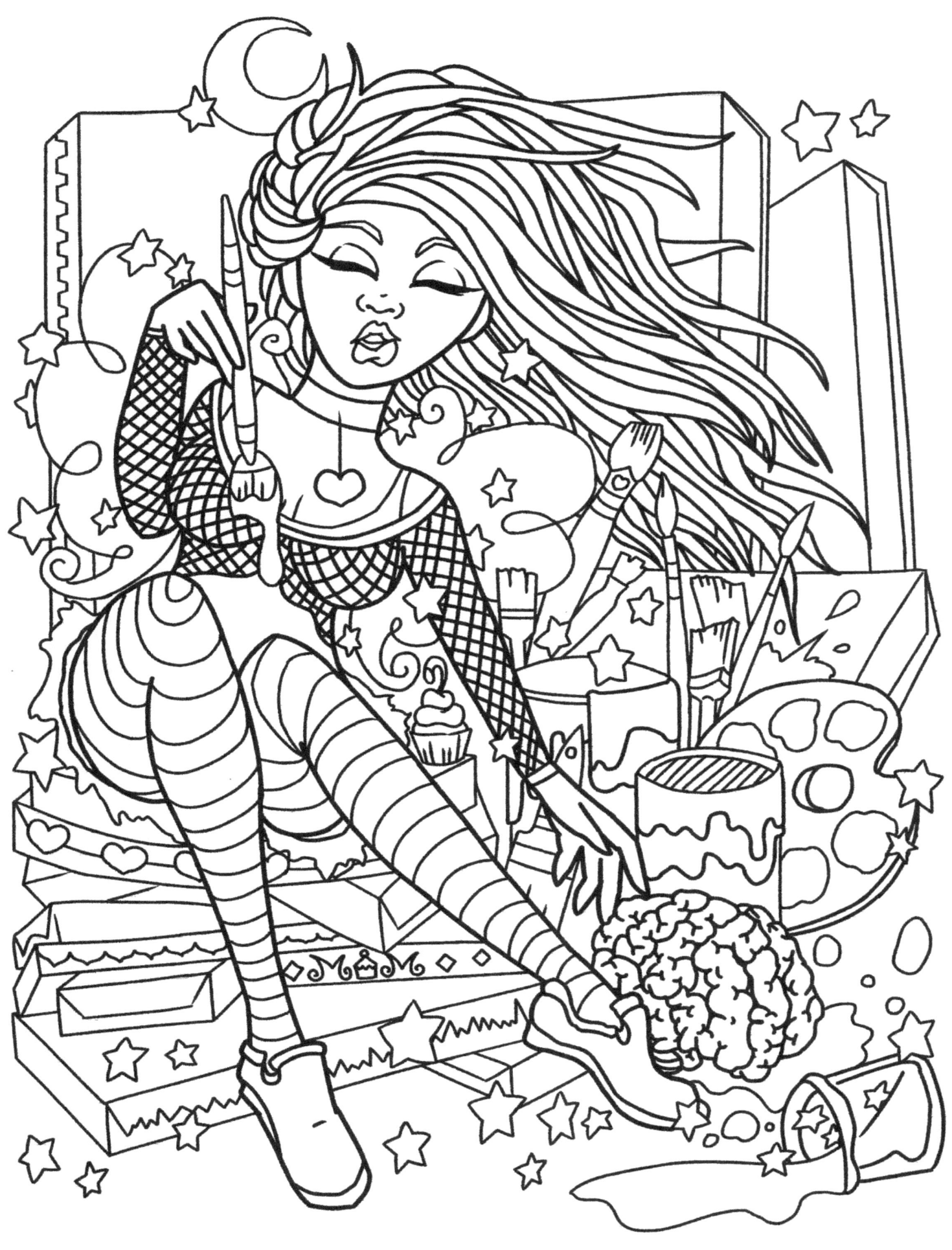

Ms. Muffintop's

Color Test Page!!!

Test your colors here!